Try It My

A **FULL CIRCLE** BOOK

OSHO titles published by FULL CIRCLE

OSHO — Zen Series
- Walking in Zen, Sitting in Zen
- So Lost and So at Home
- Ah, This!

Other Osho Titles
- Tantra : The Supreme Understanding
- Won't you Join the Dance?
- Priests & Politicians — The Mafia of the Soul
- Walk without Feet
- My Diamond Days with Osho
- India, My Love (HC • Gift Edition)
- The Goose is Out
- Words from a Man of No Words!
- Sex, Money and Power
- Be Here Now (Audio)
- A New Vision of Women's Liberation
- The Rebel: The Very Salt of the Earth
- I Teach Religiousness, Not Religion

OSHO — Love Series
- Love and Hate
- Love and Relationship
- Love and Freedom
- Love Yourself
- Love and Being

OSHO — Meditation Series
- Surrender to Existence
- Love is a Free Bird
- Stranger to the Earth
- Alone We Fly
- I Teach Fearlessness
- A Dewdrop in the Ocean
- Say Yes!
- Life is a Gift
- Be a Lamp unto Yourself
- Live Dangerously
- Become One with Yourself
- Meditation — An Ecstasy

Try It My Way

OSHO

TRY IT MY WAY

Published by
FULL CIRCLE *PUBLISHING*
18-19, Dilshad Garden, G.T. Road, Delhi-110 095
Tel: 228 2467, 229 7792 Fax: 228 2332 e-mail: fullcircle@vsnl.com

Copyright © 2001 Osho International Foundation, All rights reserved

Originally published in English as
'Ah, This!', chapters 5-8
Copyright © 1982 Osho International Foundation, All rights reserved.

Osho® is a registered trademark of Osho International Foundation,
used under license.

Coordinated by Swami Amano Manish

First Edition, 2001

ISBN 81-7621-087-0

For sale in India only

No part of this book may be reproduced or transmitted in any form or by any means electronic or mechanical including photocopying or recording or by any information storage and retrieval system without permission in writing from the Publisher.

Printed at Nu Tech Photolithographers, Delhi-110095

PRINTED IN INDIA

Contents

See Right At Once
3

Try It My Way
31

Take No Notice
61

Not Knowing Is The Most Intimate
91

*The discourses in this book,
based on Zen stories
and questions and answers
were given by Osho
at the Osho International Commune,
Pune, India
January 3 - 10, 1980*

*Four of these discourses form this volume in
your hands, "Try It My Way". The other
four discourses you will find in a book
called "Ah, This!".*

The Zen stories in this book are excerpted from:
ZEN AND JAPANESE CULTURE, Bollingen Series
LXIV, Copyright 1959, by Daisetz T. Suzuki, reprinted
with the kind permission of the publishers, Princeton
University Press, Princeton, N.J.

and

CH'AN AND ZEN TEACHING, Series One, edited,
translated and explained by Lu K'uan Yu (Charles Luk),
Hutchinson Publishing Group Ltd., London.

Dogo had a disciple called Soshin. When Soshin was taken in as a novice, it was perhaps natural of him to expect lessons in Zen from his teacher the way a schoolboy is taught at school. But Dogo gave him no special lessons on the subject, and this bewildered and disappointed Soshin.

One day he said to the Master, "It is some time since I came here, but not a word has been given me regarding the essence of the Zen teaching."

Dogo replied, "Since your arrival I have ever been giving you lessons on the matter of Zen discipline."

"What kind of lesson could it have been?"

"When you bring me a cup of tea in the morning, I take it; when you serve me a meal, I accept it; when you bow to me, I return it with a nod. How else do you expect to be taught in the discipline of Zen?"

Soshin hung his head for a while, pondering the puzzling words of the Master.

The Master said, "If you want to see, see right at once. When you begin to think, you miss the point."

See Right At Once

Sujata has written to me:
How odd of God to choose the Jews!

Sujata,

GOD HAS A TREMENDOUS SENSE OF HUMOR! RELIGION REMAINS SOMEthing dead without a sense of humor as a foundation to it. God would not have been able to create the world if he had no sense of humor. God is not serious at all. Seriousness is a state of dis-ease; humor is health. Love, laughter, life, they are aspects of the same energy.

But for centuries people have been told that God is very serious. These people were pathological. They created a serious God, they projected a serious God, out of their own pathology. And we have worshipped these people as saints. They were not saints. They needed great awakening; they were fast asleep in their seriousness. They needed laughter — that would have helped them more than all their prayers and fasting; that would have cleansed their souls in a far better way than all their ascetic practices. They did not need more scriptures, more theologies; they needed only the capacity to laugh at the beautiful absurdity of life. It is ecstatically absurd. It is not a rational phenomenon; it is utterly irrational.

Moses went up the mountain. After a long time God appeared. "Hello, Moses. Good to see you. Sorry you had to wait, but I think you will feel it was worth it because I have something very special for you today."

Moses thought for a second and then said, "Oh, no, Lord, really. Thank you, but I don't need anything right now. Some other time perhaps."

"Moses, this is free," said the Lord.

"Then," said Moses, "give me ten!"

That's how the Jews got the Ten Commandments.

Sujata, Zen has something Jewish in it. It is really very puzzling why Zen did not appear in the Jewish world. But the Chinese also have a tremendous sense of humor. Zen is not Indian, remember. Of course, the origin is in Gautam the Buddha, but it went through a tremendous transformation passing through the Chinese consciousness.

There are a few very wise people who think that Zen is more a rebellion against the Indian seriousness than a continuity of it. And they have a point there; a certain truth is there. Lao Tzu is more Jewish than Hindu — he can laugh. Chuang Tzu has written such beautiful and absurd stories; nobody can conceive of an enlightened person writing such stories, which can only be called, at the best, entertainment. But entertainment can become the door to enlightenment.

Zen is originally connected with Buddha, but the color and the flavor that came to it came through Lao Tzu, Chuang Tzu, Lieh Tzu and the Chinese consciousness. And then it blossomed in Japan; it came to its ultimate peak in Japan. Japan also has a great quality: of taking life playfully. The consciousness of Japan is very colorful.

Zen could have happened in the Jewish world too. Something like it really *did* happen — that is Hassidism. This story must have come from Jewish sources, although it is about Jesus. But Christians have no sense of humor. And Jesus was never a Christian, remember. He was born a Jew, he lived as a Jew, he died as a Jew.

> Jesus is hanging on the cross singing, "Da-di-li-da-dum-dei...."
> Suddenly Peter hisses from underneath, "Hey, Jesus!"
> Jesus goes on, "Da-li-di-dum-da-dum-da-dei..."
> Peter, now more urgently, "Hey, Jesus, stop it!"
> Jesus continues happily with "Di-duah-duah...."
> Finally Peter yells, "For God's sake, Jesus, cut it out! Tourists are coming!"

Try to understand Zen through laughter, not through prayer. Try to understand Zen through flowers, butterflies, sun, moon, children, people in all their absurdities. Watch this whole panorama of life, all these colors, the whole spectrum.

Zen is not a doctrine, it is not a dogma. It is growing into an insight. It is a vision — very light-hearted, not serious at all.

Be light-hearted, light-footed. Be of light step. Don't carry religion like a burden. And don't expect religion to be a teaching; it is not. It is certainly a discipline, but not a teaching at all. Teaching has to be imposed upon you from the outside and teaching can only reach to your mind, never to your heart, and never, never to the very center of your being. Teaching remains intellectual. It is an answer to human curiosity, and curiosity is not a true search.

The student remains outside the temple of Zen because he remains curious. He wants to know answers and there are none. He has some stupid questions to be answered: "Who made the world? Why did he make the world?" And so on and so forth. "How many heavens are there and how many hells? And how many angels can dance on the point of a needle? And is the world infinite or finite? Are there many lives or only one?" These are all curiosities — good for a student of philosophy but not good for a disciple.

A disciple has to drop curiosity. Curiosity is something very superficial. Even if those questions are answered, nothing will have happened to your being; you will remain the same. Yes, you will have more information, and out of that information you will create new questions. Each question answered brings ten more new questions; the answer creates ten more new questions.

If somebody says, "God created the world," then the question is, "Why did he create the world? And why a world like this? — so miserable. If he is omnipotent, omniscient, omnipresent, could he not see what he was doing? Why did he create pain, disease, death?" Now, so many questions....

Philosophy is an exercise in futility.

A student comes out of curiosity. Unless he becomes a disciple he will not become aware that curiosity is a vicious circle. You ask one question, you are given the answer, the answer brings ten more new questions, and so on and so forth. And the tree becomes bigger and bigger; thicker and thicker is the foliage. And finally the philosopher has only questions and no answers at all.

Surrounded by all those stupid questions ... stupid I call them because they have no answers; stupid I call them because they are born out of childish curiosity. When one is surrounded by all those questions and there is no answer, one loses sharpness, one loses clarity, one is clouded. And one is no more intelligent. The more intellectual one becomes, the less intelligent he is.

The professor who had committed his wife to a mental institution was talking to the chief of staff. "How will we know when my wife is well again, doctor?"

"We have a simple test we give all our patients," he replied. "We put a hose into a trough, turn on the water, give the patient a bucket, and tell him to empty out the trough."

"What does that prove?" enquired the professor.

"Elementary, sir," the doctor assured him. "Any sane person will turn off the hose."

"Isn't science wonderful!" he replied. "I never would have thought of that!"

He must be a professor of philosophy; he can't be less than that.

The professor only knows questions. He is lost in the jungle of questions. The philosopher remains immature. Maturity is of consciousness, not of intellectuality. It is not of knowledge, it is of innocence.

Yes: *Not to know is the most intimate.* And to function out of that not-knowing is to function in an enlightened way. To respond out of not-knowing is to respond like a Buddha. That is true response because it is not clouded, not distorted, not contaminated, not polluted and poisoned by your mind and your past. It is fresh, it is young, it is new. It arises to the challenge of the present. It is always in synchronicity with the new, with the present. And the present is always new, it is always moving — it is dynamic. All your answers are static, and life is dynamic.

Try It My Way

HENCE ZEN IS NOT INTERESTED IN ANSWERS — OR IN QUESTIONS. IT IS not interested in teaching at all. It is not a philosophy; it is a totally different way of looking at things, at life, at existence, at oneself, at others. Yes, it is a discipline.

Discipline simply means a methodology of becoming more centered, of becoming more alert, of becoming more aware, of bringing more meditativeness to your being; not functioning through the head, not even through the heart, but functioning from the very core of your being, from the very innermost core, from the center of your being, from your totality. It is not a reaction — reaction comes from the past — it is a response. Response is always *in* the present, *to* the present.

Zen gives you a discipline to become a mirror so that you can reflect that which is. All that is needed is a thoughtless awareness.

The first thing to be dropped is curiosity, because curiosity will keep you tethered to the futile. It will keep you being a student; it will never allow you to become a disciple.

Boris, who was from Russia, had been in America only a few months. He did not speak English very well.

One day he was asked, "Boris, what is it that you are most anxious to see in America?"

"Well," replied Boris, "I weesh most to meet the most famous Mrs. Beech, who had so many sons in the last war."

Get it? He must have heard all the Americans calling each other "sonofabitch, sonofabitch..." so he is very much interested, anxious, curious, to know about Mrs. Beech, the famous Mrs. Beech.

Curiosity is always like that. It is foolish, but it can keep you tethered to the mind. And don't think that there is some curiosity which is spiritual, metaphysical. No, nothing like that exists; all curiosity is the same. Whether you enquire about "the famous Mrs. Beech" or you enquire about God it is all the same. Enquiry from the mind will have the same quality — of childishness.

There is a totally different kind of enquiry that arises from the deeper recesses of your being.

Zen is interested in discipline, not in teaching. It wants you to be more alert so you can see more clearly. It does not give you the answer; it gives you the *eyes* to see. What is the use of telling a blind man what light is and all the theories about light? It is futile. You are simply being stupid by answering the curiosity of a blind man. What is urgently needed is treatment of his eyes. He needs an operation, he needs new eyes, he needs medicine. That is discipline.

Buddha has said: "I am a physician, not a philosopher." And Zen is absolutely a treatment. It is the greatest treatment that has come to humanity, out of the work of thousands of enlightened people — very refined. It can help to open up your eyes. It can help you to feel again, to be sensitive to the reality. It can give you eyes and ears. It can give you a soul. But it is not interested in answers. Meditate over this beautiful story:

> *Dogo had a disciple called Soshin. When Soshin was taken in as a novice, it was perhaps natural of him to expect lessons in Zen from his teacher the way a schoolboy is taught at school.*

Try It My Way

YES, IT IS NATURAL IN A WAY, BECAUSE THAT'S HOW WE ARE CONDItioned. Knowledge is given to us in the form of questions and answers. From the primary school to the university that's how we are taught, conditioned, hypnotized. And naturally, after one third of your life is wasted in that way, you become accustomed to it. Then you start asking profound questions in the same way as one asks, "How much is two plus two?" You start asking about love, life, God, meditation — in the same way!

In fact, even that ordinary question is not answerable. If you ask the real mathematicians, even this simple question "How much is two plus two?" is not answerable, because sometimes it is five and sometimes it is three. It is very rarely four. It is an exception that two plus two comes to be four, very exceptional, for the simple reason that two things are never the same. It is an abstraction: you add two and two and you say four.

Two persons and two persons are four *different* persons, *so* different that you cannot create an abstraction out of them. Even two leaves and two other leaves are so different that you cannot simply call them four leaves; they are not the same. Their weights are different, their colors are different, their shapes are different, their tastes are different. No two things in the world are the same. So how can two plus two be four? It is just an abstraction; it is lower mathematics. Higher mathematics knows that this is only utilitarian, it is not a truth. Mathematics is an invention of man; it is a workable lie.

What to say about love, which goes beyond all mathematics and all logic? In love, one plus one becomes one, not two. In deep love, the twoness disappears. Mathematics is transcended; it becomes irrelevant. In deep love, two persons are no more two persons, they become one. They start feeling, functioning, as one unit, as one organic unity, as one orgasmic joy. Mathematics won't do, logic won't do, chemistry won't do, biology won't do, physiology won't do. Love is something which has to be experienced in a totally different way. It cannot be taught in the ordinary ways of teaching; it cannot become part of pedagogy.

But the disciple, Soshin, was a novice, a newcomer.

> *...it was perhaps natural of him to expect lessons in Zen from his teacher the way a schoolboy is taught at school.*

It is natural in a state of unconsciousness.

Remember, there are two natures. One is when you are asleep; then many things are natural. Somebody insults you, you become angry, and that is *natural* — but only in unconsciousness, in sleep. You insult the Buddha, he does not become angry — that is higher nature, a totally different kind of nature. He is functioning from a different center altogether. He may feel compassion for you, not anger. He functions through awareness, you function through unawareness.

In sleep you cannot do anything of any value, you cannot do anything valuable. Whatsoever you do is all dream. You imagine, you think you are doing good.

Just the other day somebody asked: "I want to do good, I want to *be* good. Osho, help me."

I cannot help you directly to do good or to be good; I can help you only indirectly. I can help you only to be more meditative. And on the surface it may seem that your question is about something else and my answer is totally different: you want to be good and I talk about meditation. How are they related? If you are asleep you may *think* you are doing good, you may do harm. You may *think* you are doing harm, you may do good. In your sleep everything is possible.

You will become a do-gooder — and do-gooders are the most mischievous people. We have suffered much from these do-gooders. They don't know who they are, they don't know any silent state of consciousness, they are not aware, but they go on doing good. What to say about good? A sleepy person cannot even be certain of doing harm. He may think he is doing harm and the result may be totally different.

That's how acupuncture was discovered. A man wanted to kill somebody; he shot him with an arrow. And that man, the victim, had suffered his whole life from a headache. The arrow hit him on the leg and the headache disappeared, totally disappeared. He was puzzled.

He went to his physician saying, "You have not been able to treat me and my enemy has treated me. He wanted to kill me, but something went wrong — my headache has disappeared. I am grateful to him."

Then the physicians started thinking about it, how it happened. That's what acupuncturists go on doing now.

You can go to Abhiyana. You may have a headache and he may start putting needles all over your body. Those needle points were discovered because of this accident. Five thousand years have passed; in these five thousand years acupuncture has developed tremendously. Now there is much scientific support for it.

In Soviet Russia they are working on acupuncture very seriously because it has great potential: it can cure almost all diseases. Those needles can change the currents of your body electricity.

See Right At Once

That man must have suffered from too much electricity in the head. The arrow hit a certain meridian, a certain electric current in his leg, and the electricity changed its course; it was no longer going to the head. Hence the headache disappeared.

Now, the man who wanted to do harm did a great, beneficial act for the whole of humanity — not only for that man — because in these five thousand years, millions of people have been helped by acupuncture. The whole credit goes to that unknown person who wanted to kill.

In your unconsciousness it is difficult to decide what the outcome will be. You move in a dark dark night. All is accidental.

Sindenburg had lived a virtuous life; he was even president of the synagogue. But when he entered heaven the angel in charge said, "You can't stay here."

"Why?" asked Sindenburg. "I always tried to be a good man."

"That is it," explained the angel. "Everyone here was a good man, but they all committed at least one sin. Since you didn't sin at all, the rest of the souls will resent you."

"But," protested Sindenburg, "isn't there something I can do?"

"Well," considered the angel, "you can have six more hours on earth to commit a sin, but you must do somebody a real injury."

Sindenburg went back to earth and suddenly he saw a middle-aged woman looking at him. They started talking; she invited him home with her. Soon they were making love like two teenagers.

Six hours later Sindenburg said, "I am sorry, but I have to go now."

"Listen!" cried the woman. "I never married or even had

a man. You just gave me the best time I had in my whole life. What a good deed you did today!"

Now he came to do some real injury and what he has really done is a good deed. The woman is immensely happy and grateful. And those six hours are gone; now there is no more time left. Again he will be in trouble!

In sleep you cannot do good — you cannot even do bad! All is accidental. And when a person comes to a Master he comes almost fast asleep. He comes out of curiosity, accidentally. He expects much, and his expectations are natural in his state.

He expected *lessons in Zen...*

Now that is absolutely foolish: there are no lessons in Zen. Zen, in the first place, is not a teaching but a device to awaken you. It is not information, it is not knowledge. It is a method to shake you up, to wake you up. Teaching means you are fast asleep and somebody goes on talking about what awakening is — and you go on snoring and he goes on talking. *You* are asleep, *he* is asleep; otherwise he will not talk to you. At least when he sees that you are snoring he will not talk to you.

When I was a student at university I had a great teacher, a very well-known philosopher. For three years nobody had joined his class — he was the head of the department. And people were afraid to join his class because he was a nonstop talker. Sometimes two hours, three hours, four hours .... And he had this condition: he would say to every student, "If you want to participate in *my* classes, if you want to take *my* subject, then this must be remembered: that I can *start* my lecture when the period starts, but I cannot stop when the period is over. Unless I am totally finished with the subject ... and how can it be manage´ within forty minutes? Sometimes it takes two hours, sometimes it takes only half an hour. So whenever it is finished, that is the end."

He also told me the same. I wanted to join his class — I was intrigued by the old man. He said, "Listen! Don't blame me later on. Sometimes I speak for four hours; five hours also I have spoken."

I said, "You don't be worried about that. I can speak longer than you." And I told him, "Remember that when I start speaking I forget who is the teacher and who is the student. I don't care! So you also keep it in mind that if *I* start speaking you cannot stop me.

"And secondly: the time of your periods is such that those are the hours when I sleep. From twelve to two I must sleep; that I have done my whole life. I can sleep longer — I have slept from eleven to five, the whole day — but this much is absolutely necessary, that I cannot miss. So I will sleep — you can go on talking."

He said, "How can you sleep when I am talking?"

I said, "I use earplugs! You go on talking. I am not concerned with your talk at all, that is up to you. You enjoy it to your heart's content — I will be sleeping. And you cannot object to that."

He agreed to my condition, I agreed to his condition. And that's how we became great friends: he would speak and I would sleep.

Now this person must be fast asleep himself, otherwise why ... because I was the only student in his class! To whom was he talking? He was unburdening himself. And he was very happy to find a student who would at least remain in the class — although asleep, but at least he was there.

This is what goes on in the whole world! Priests are asleep talking to their congregations. Professors are asleep talking to their students — metaphysically asleep; I am not talking about the ordinary sleep. Metaphysically everybody is snoring.

Zen is not a teaching, because it knows you are asleep. The primary thing is not to teach you; the primary thing is to wake you up. Zen is an alarm.

But Soshin naturally expected some lessons in Zen from his teacher *the way a schoolboy is taught at school.*

Remember, if Zen is not a teaching then you cannot call the Zen Master a teacher either. He is not a teacher, he is a Master. And there is a great difference between a teacher and a Master. But when you first come in close contact with a Master you think of him as a teacher — maybe a great teacher, but still you think in terms of his being a teacher. And the reason is in your expectation that he is teaching something: that he is teaching great philosophy, that he is teaching great truths.

No, a real Master is not a teacher: a real Master is an awakener. His function is totally different from a teacher; his function is far more difficult. And only very few people can stay with a Master because to wake up after millions of lives is not an ordinary feat; it is a miracle. And to allow somebody to wake you up needs great trust, great surrender.

So in Zen, first, people are accepted only as novices, as beginners. Only when the Master sees some quality in them which can be awakened, when he sees something very potential, then they are accepted and initiated into higher things. Otherwise they remain novices for years, doing small things: cleaning the floor, cooking the food, chopping wood, carrying water from the well. And the Master goes on watching and he goes on helping them to become a little more alert while they are chopping wood, while they are carrying water from the well, while they are cleaning the floor.

You will see here in this commune at least one thousand sannyasins doing different kinds of things. When Indians come here for the first time they are puzzled, because their idea of an ashram, of a religious commune, is totally different. People should be sitting praying, doing *bhajan*. They can't conceive that people should be working, cooking food, weaving, doing pottery, painting, photography, creating music, poetry, dancing. They can't believe their eyes when they see the commune for the first time. They come with certain expectations. And they want you to look serious, religious, holy. And you look so joyous! You look so loving, so warm. They expect you to be utterly cold — as cold as corpses. And you are so warm and so loving and so alive that they are shocked for the first time.

Zen does not believe that people should just live a holy life, a virtuous life, doing nothing — just turning beads or repeating some mantra. Zen believes in creativity. Zen believes in the ordinary world. It wants to transform the mundane into the sacred.

So the first message given to the beginners is to start work but be alert. And it is easier to be alert while you are working than while you are simply chanting a mantra, because when you are chanting a mantra every possibility is that the mantra will function as a tranquilizer. When you repeat a single word again and again it creates sleep because it creates boredom. When you repeat a certain word again and again it changes your inner chemistry. It is one of the ancientmost ways of falling asleep.

If you cannot fall asleep in the night, if you suffer from sleeplessness, then methods like Maharishi Mahesh Yogi's Transcendental Meditation are perfectly good. That method has nothing to do with meditation; it is neither meditation nor transcendental. It is simply a non-medicinal tranquilizer. It is good as far as it can bring sleep and without any drug — I appreciate it — but it has nothing to do with meditation.

You can repeat your own name again and again and you don't need to pay the fees to anybody and you don't need any initiation. Just repeat your own name; repeat it fast so that nothing else enters your mind, only your name resounds. Repeat loudly inside so that from your toes to the head it is resounding inside. Soon you will get bored, fed up. And that is the moment when you start falling asleep because there seems to be no other escape.

All mothers know it. It is one of the ancientmost methods women have been using with their children, on their children. They didn't call it Transcendental Meditation; they used to call it "lullaby." The child tosses and turns, but the mother goes on repeating the same line again and again. And finding no other escape outside, the child escapes inside; that means he falls asleep. He says, "I am so fed up that unless I fall asleep, this woman is not going to stop." And soon he learns: the moment he falls asleep the woman stops, so it becomes a conditioning; then it becomes a conditioned reflex. Slowly slowly, the woman just repeats the line one or two times and the child is fast asleep.

This you can do to yourself. It is a process of auto-hypnosis; good as far as sleep is concerned but it has nothing to do with meditation. In fact, it is just the opposite of meditation, because meditation brings awareness and this method brings sleep. Hence I appreciate it as a technique for sleep, but I am totally against it if it is taught to people as a method of meditation.

Soshin expected *lessons in Zen from his teacher the way a schoolboy is taught at school.*

This is *your* story. This is everybody's story. Each seeker comes with such expectations.

Sometimes foolish people come to me and they ask: "What is your teaching in short?" "Which of your books contains your total teaching?"

I have no teaching! That's why so many books are possible. Otherwise how can so many books be possible? If you have a certain teaching, then one or two books will do. That's why I can go on talking for ever, because I have no teaching. Every teaching will sooner or later be exhausted; I cannot be exhausted. There is no beginning and no end... we are always in the middle. I am not a teacher.

Everybody grows physically but psychologically remains a child. Your psychological age is never more than thirteen, even less than that. It was a shock when it was discovered for the first time in the First World War that man's average psychological age is only twelve or thirteen at the most. That means you may be seventy but your mind is only thirteen. So if somebody looks at your body you look so old, so experienced, but if somebody looks into your mind you are carrying the same childish mind still.

Your God is nothing but a projected father; it is a father fixation. You cannot live without the idea of a father. Maybe your actual father is dead and you cannot conceive of yourself without a father. You need an imaginary father in heaven who takes care of you, who looks after you. And, certainly, the ordinary father is bound to die one day or other so you need a heavenly father who is eternal, who will never die, so he will become your safety and security.

Once somebody asked George Gurdjieff, "Why do all the religions teach: Respect your parents?"

Gurdjieff said, "For a simple reason: if you respect your parents you will respect God, because God is nothing but the ultimate parent. If you don't respect your parents you will not be bothered with God either."

A great insight: God is the great father; you are just small children searching for a lost father, searching for a lost childhood, searching for the security of childhood. Your behavior is childish.

A young father was shopping at a department store with his daughter when the little girl suddenly said, "Daddy, I gotta go."

"Not right now," replied the father.

"I gotta go *now!*" shouted the girl.

To avoid a crisis a saleslady stepped up and said, "That's all right, sir, I will take her."

The saleslady and the little girl went off hurriedly, hand in hand. On their return, Tony looked at his daughter and said, "Did you thank the nice lady for being so kind?"

"Why should I thank her?" retorted the little girl. "She had to go too!"

Just watch your reactions and you will be surprised: they are childish. Your manners, howsoever sophisticated from the outside, deep down are childish. Your prayers, your church-going, are *all* childish.

Zen is not concerned with your childish state of mind. It has no desire to nourish it any more. Its concern is maturity; it wants you to become mature, it wants you to become ripe. Hence it has no idea of God — no father in the sky. It leaves you totally alone because only in aloneness is maturity possible. It leaves you totally in insecurity. It gives you no security, no guarantee. It gives you all kinds of insecurities to move into.

And that's what sannyas is also: a quantum leap into

insecurity, a quantum leap into the unknown, because only with that encounter will you become mature. And maturity is freedom, maturity is liberation.

> *But Dogo gave him no special lessons on the subject...*

There are none.

> *...and this bewildered and disappointed Soshin.*

Naturally. He was expecting and expecting and waiting, and no special lessons were given. He wanted a few simple principles so he could cling to them, so that he could hold onto them, so that they would become his treasure, his knowledge. And the Master had not given any special lesson. Naturally he was disappointed. If you are expecting anything you are bound to be disappointed. Expectation always brings disappointment, frustration.

> *One day he said to the Master, "It is some time since I came here, but not a word has been given me regarding the essence of the Zen teaching."*

People are in a hurry. I have come to know people who have meditated three days, and on the fourth day they ask, "Three days we have been meditating, why has nothing happened yet?"

As if they are obliging existence by meditating for so long — three days, one hour every day; that means three hours. And if you actually look, in their meditation they were just daydreaming; with closed eyes they were daydreaming. They call it meditation! And just because for three days they have been sitting for one hour — with great difficulty, somehow managing, great noise inside, no silence, no peace, no consciousness, just desires, thoughts, memories, imagination, constant traffic, a crowd — then they come on the fourth day saying, "Osho, what is happening? Three days have passed and nothing has happened yet."

Time should not be taken into account at all — three years, not even three lives. You should not think in terms of time, because the phenomenon of meditation is non-temporal. It can happen any moment, it can happen *right* now; it may take years, it may take lives. It all depends on your intensity, on your sincerity, and it all depends on your totality.

A pretty young woman stepped onto a crowded streetcar, and seeing that all the seats were taken she asked, "Would one of you gentlemen make room for a pregnant woman?"

A middle-aged man quickly stood up and gave her his seat. After she was seated he solicitously asked her, "How long have you been pregnant?"

"About fifteen minutes, and God, am I tired!"

Fifteen minutes pregnant! Even that is okay, but three days of meditation is even more stupid.

> *Soshin said one day to the Master...*

There must be some anger, frustration, disappointment. Has he chosen a wrong person to be with? No special teaching has been given yet — and the ego always wants something special.

> *"It is some time since I came here," he said, "but not a word has been given me regarding the essence of the Zen teaching."*

In the first place, there is no Zen teaching as such. Zen is a method of awakening, not a theology. It does not talk about God: it forces you into God. It hits you in many ways so that you can be awakened into God. To be asleep is to be in the world: to be awake is to be in God. Methods are there, devices are there, but no teaching at all.

In a little New Mexico town, a pretty young tourist overheard a virile Navajo saying "Chance!" to every passing female.

Finally her curiosity got the better of her and she walked up to him and said "Hello," to which he answered "Chance!"

"I thought all Indians said 'How!'"

"I know how — just want chance!" he replied.

All teachings are concerned about how to do it, why to do it, for what purpose, for what goal. Zen simply gives you a chance, an opportunity, a certain context, a space in which you can become awakened. And that's exactly *my* work here: to create an opportunity, a space, a context, where you are *bound* to be awakened, where you *cannot* go on sleeping forever.

> *Dogo replied, "Since your arrival I have ever been giving you lessons on the matter of Zen discipline."*
>
> *"What kind of lesson could it have been?"*

Now Soshin is even more puzzled and bewildered because the Master says:

> *"Since your arrival I have ever been giving you lessons on the matter of Zen discipline."*

Strange are the ways of the real Masters. Indirect are their ways, subtle are their ways. Remember, he does not say "on Zen teaching"; he says "on Zen discipline — on the matter of Zen discipline."

> *"What kind of lesson could it have been?"*
>
> *"When you bring me a cup of tea in the morning, I take it; when you serve me a meal, I accept it; when you bow to me, I return it with a nod."*

The Master is saying, "Have you observed me?" That is the essential core of Zen: watching, observing, being aware. The Master is saying, "When you bring a cup of tea in the morning for me, have you watched me — how I take it, with what gratitude? Have you watched me — how I accept it with great awareness? It is not just tea!"

Nothing is ordinary in the eyes of Zen; everything is extraordinary because everything is divine. Zen Masters have transformed ordinary things like tea-drinking into religious ceremonies.

The tea ceremony is a great meditation; it takes hours. In every Zen monastery there is a separate place for the tea ceremony, a temple — a temple for tea! And when people are invited by the Master they go to the temple in absolute silence. The temple is surrounded by rocks or a rock garden.

Sanantano has just now made a small rock garden around my room, with a small waterfall. He has placed the rocks in such a beautiful way — he seems to have the insight, seems to have a communion with the rocks. The rocks have come alive and they don't seem to be just put any way, haphazardly; they seem to be in a deep harmony.

Now, Sanantano is going to create many rock gardens in the new commune so you can sit by those rocks...and small bamboo huts for the tea ceremony.

See Right At Once

And when a person goes — when the Master invites someone for tea — he takes a bath, he meditates, he cools himself down. He prepares himself because it is no ordinary occasion: an invitation from the Master. Then he walks the rocky path with full awareness, slowly. The closer he comes to the temple, the more alert he becomes. He becomes alert to the birds singing. He becomes alert to the flowers, their colors, their fragrance. And as he comes closer to the tearoom he starts hearing the noise of the samovar. He goes in. The shoes have to be left outside. He enters very silently, bows down to the Master, sits quietly in a corner listening to the samovar, the humming sound of the samovar ... and the subtle fragrance of tea filling the room. It is a prayerful moment.

Then cups and saucers are given. The Master himself gives those cups and saucers...the way he gives. He pours the tea ... the way he pours. Then they all sip the tea silently. It has to be sipped with tremendous awareness; then it becomes a meditation.

And if tea-drinking can become a meditation, then anything can become a meditation — cooking or washing your clothes, any activity can be transformed into meditation. And the real sannyasin, the real seeker, will transform all his acts into meditation. Only then, when meditation spreads over all your life, not only when you are awake in the day — slowly slowly it starts penetrating and permeating your being in sleep too — when it becomes just part of you, like breathing, like your heartbeat, then, only, have you attained to the discipline, to the essential discipline of Zen.

The Master said:

> *"When you bring me a cup of tea in the morning...*

"Have you observed or not? Are you asleep or awake? Can't you see the way I take it? *When you serve me a meal* ...can't you see the way I accept it, with great gratitude, as if you have brought a treasure?

"...when you bow to me, I return it with a nod.

"Have I ever missed? Has it ever been noticed by you that I have not responded immediately? If you have been watching, then this is the real matter of Zen discipline. Do the same, do likewise!

"How else do you expect to be taught in the discipline of Zen?"

But you don't watch, you don't see. You go on rushing, doing things somehow, mechanically. And you go on falling into pitfalls, the *same* pitfalls again and again.

A negro walks into a white bar with three friends, goes up to the barman and bets him $25 he can lick his own eye.

The barman thinks, "God-damned stupid negro, nobody can lick his own eye," so he bets him the $25. The negro takes out his glass eye and licks it and then bets the barman another $25 he can bite his other eye.

The barman thinks, "Oh boy, is this negro ever dumb! Nobody could come in here with two glass eyes," and takes him up on the bet. The negro takes his false teeth out and bites the other eye and the barman turns red with anger: "Smartass negro!"

Then the negro says, "I will bet you another $25...."

"Wait a minute," says the barman. "No way. You think I'm stupid?"

"Oh, come on," says the negro. "I'll bet you double or nothing I can piss in that shot glass on the table on the other side of the room."

See Right At Once

The barman stops, ponders a while and says, "Okay, even a stupid god-damned negro couldn't do that! You're on. I'll bet you double or nothing!"

The negro proceeds to piss all over the bar, the floor, everywhere. The barman starts laughing like hell, and wiping it up, says, "Boy, negro, you are really dumb to think you could piss that far!"

And the negro replies, "I'm not so dumb — see those three dudes over there? I bet them $300 I could piss all over the bar and you would wipe it up laughing!"

Man goes on doing the same; maybe a slightly different situation, but nothing very different. If you are asleep, if you are unconscious, you cannot watch, you cannot observe that again another pitfall ... that again you are going into another mistake, another error, that you are again stumbling. Maybe it is a little bit different, because in life nothing is ever the same, but thousands of times you fall and still you don't learn the single thing worth learning. You learn all kinds of things in life except the one thing which can transform you, and that is the art of awareness.

> *Soshin hung his head for a while, pondering the puzzling words of the Master.*
>
> *The Master said, "If you want to see, see right at once. When you begin to think, you miss the point."*

These are tremendously significant words:

> *"If you want to see, see right at once. When you begin to think, you miss the point."*

Try It My Way

BECAUSE THINKING IS ONLY A WAY OF MISSING THE POINT. WHEN YOU hear the truth, *see* it immediately. Don't say, "I will think it over." Don't take notes saying, "Back home I will ponder over it." You are missing the whole point! Truth has an immediacy, and you are postponing it by thinking. And what can you think about truth? And whatsoever you think is going to be wrong. Truth is truth and untruth is untruth. You cannot make an untruth truth by thinking for years, and you cannot make a truth untruth by thinking for years. Nothing can be done about it; your thinking is absolutely irrelevant. *See* it. Seeing is relevant; thinking is not relevant.

That's why in the East we don't have any word to translate the English word "philosophy". We have a word, *darshan*, which is ordinarily used as a translation for philosophy but it is not right to do that. *Darshan* means seeing, and philosophy means thinking — and there is such a tremendous difference, such a vast difference, between the two. What greater difference can there be between two things — seeing and thinking?

Darshan simply means seeing. It is *not* thinking, it is awareness. Silently alert you sit by the side of the Master. He says something — or *shows* something rather — and you see it! If you are silent and aware you are bound to see it, you cannot miss it. If you hang your head and you start thinking, you have forgotten about the Master; you are lost in your own words. You are translating the Master into your own words — and you cannot translate those heights, those depths. And whatsoever you translate will be something utterly different from what the Master has said.

See Right At Once

Three Frenchmen, while practicing their English, got around to discussing the wife of a friend who was childless.

"She is unbearable," said one.

"No, that is the wrong word. She is inconceivable."

"No, no, you are both wrong," said the third. "What you mean is she is impregnable."

Now, you can go on thinking....When the Master speaks, he speaks from the heights of awareness — and you listen in the darkness of your valley. Don't translate and don't try to figure it out, what he is saying. Just listen.

Just the other day somebody asked: "Listening to you unquestioningly, accepting it, isn't it a way of being conditioned by you?"

Listening silently does not mean that you are agreeing with me. It is not a question of agreement or disagreement. Listening silently does not mean that you are accepting me or rejecting me. If you are accepting you are not silent; activity is there — the activity of accepting. If you are agreeing with me that means you are already translating me. If you are rejecting me that is negative activity; if you accept me that is positive activity. And to be silent simply means no activity at all. You are simply here...just being here, only available, no question of agreeing or disagreeing.

And the beauty of truth is that the moment you hear the truth something inside you responds, says yes. It is not agreement of the mind, remember; it comes from your totality. Every fiber of your being, every cell of your body, nods in tremendous joy, "Yes!" Not that you say yes — it is not said, it is not verbalized at all. It is silently there. And when you hear some untruth, in the same way there is a no; your whole being says "no". That is not mental either.

This is a totally different approach. The West has not been able to evolve it yet; the East has evolved it. For centuries we have been working on this subtle method, polishing it, polishing it. It has become a mirror.

The East knows how to just sit in silence, without agreeing or disagreeing, because we have discovered one fundamental thing: that truth is already inside you. If you hear the truth from the outside your truth will be awakened, it will be provoked. Suddenly you will say "Yes!" — as if you had known it already. It is a recognition, it is a remembrance. You are simply being reminded by the Master about that which you have forgotten. It is not a question of agreement or disagreement — no, not at all.

I am not interested in creating beliefs in you and I am not interested in giving you any kind of ideology. My whole effort here is — as it has always been of all the Buddhas since the beginnings of time — to provoke truth in you. I know it is already there; it just needs a synchronicity. It just needs something to trigger the process of recognition in you.

The Master speaks not to give you the truth, but to help you to recognize the truth that is already within you. The Master is only a mirror. You see your own original face in deep silence, sitting by his side.

> *The Master said, "If you want to see, see right at once. When you begin to think, you miss the point."*

Try It My Way

The first question

Osho,

When I am working in the West I feel like an orange warrior, and I like it. When I am here I feel meditative, and I like it. Is the part of myself that still needs to fight an obstacle to becoming a good disciple?

Deva Majid,

A SANNYASIN HAS TO BE LIQUID, FLOWING. HE HAS NOT TO BE STONE-like, fixated. He has to be like flowing water so he can take any form. Whatsoever is the need of the moment he responds accordingly — not according to any fixed pattern, not according to any *a priori* idea of how a sannyasin should be. There is nothing like that in *my* vision of sannyas.

Never ask me how a sannyasin should be, because that will become a pattern and you will act out of the pattern. And any action out of a patterned life is wrong. One has to be loose, relaxed, so that one can respond to the situation. And situations go on changing. In the West it is different; here it is different.

So when it is needed to be a warrior, be a warrior; and

when it is needed to be meditative, be meditative. When it is needed to be an extrovert, be an extrovert; and when it is needed to be an introvert, be an introvert. This fluidity is sannyas. If you become fixated, then you are no more alive — you have become obsessed. Then you are an extrovert or an introvert, worldly or other-worldly, but you are no more my sannyasin.

My sannyasin is indescribable, as indescribable as God himself, as life itself, as love itself — as inexpressible as existence itself. A sannyasin is in total harmony with existence, so whatsoever the need of the moment, the sannyasin goes with the moment, flows with the river. He does not go upstream; he does not have any idea of how things should be. He has no "ought"; he has no commandments in his mind to be fulfilled, to be followed.

This is true discipline: discipline that brings freedom, discipline that liberates.

The second question
Osho,

I cannot drop the habit of chain-smoking. I have tried hard but I have failed always. Is it a sin to smoke?

Gurucharan,

DON'T MAKE A MOUNTAIN OUT OF A MOLEHILL! RELIGIOUS PEOPLE ARE very skillful in doing that. Now, what are you really doing when you are smoking? Just taking some smoke inside your lungs and letting it out. It is a kind of *pranayama* — filthy, dirty, but still a *pranayama!* You are doing yoga, in a stupid way. It is not a sin. It may be foolish but it is not a sin, certainly.

There is only one sin and that is unawareness, and only one virtue and that is awareness.

Do whatsoever you are doing, but remain a witness to it, and immediately the quality of your doing is transformed. I will not tell you not to smoke; that you have tried. You must have been told by many so-called saints not to smoke: "Because if you smoke you will fall into hell." God is not so stupid as your saints are. Throwing somebody into hell just because he was smoking cigarettes will be absolutely unnecessary.

One morning, Weintraub went to a restaurant and ordered bacon with his eggs. He was an orthodox Jew and his wife kept a strictly kosher home, but Weintraub felt the need just this once.

As Weintraub was about to leave the restaurant, he stopped in the door frozen with terror. The sky was filled with black clouds, there was lightning, and the ground shook with the rumble of thunder.

"Can you imagine!" he exclaimed. "All that fuss over a little piece of bacon!"

But that's what your so-called saints have been telling you down the ages, for centuries.

Smoking is unhealthy, unhygienic, but not a sin. It becomes a sin only if you are doing it unconsciously — it is not smoking that makes it a sin but unconsciousness.

Let me emphasize the fact. You can do your prayer every day unconsciously; then your prayer is a sin. You can become addicted to your prayer. If you miss the prayer one day, the whole day you will feel something is wrong, some-

Try It My Way

thing is missing, some gap. It is the same with smoking or with drinking; there is no difference in it. Your prayer has become a mechanical habit; it has become a master over you. It bosses you; you are just a servant, a slave to it. If you don't do it, it forces you to do it.

So it is not a question of smoking. You may be doing your Transcendental Meditation every day regularly, and it may be just the same. If the quality of unconsciousness is there, if mechanicalness is there, if it has become a fixed routine, if it has become a habit and you are a victim of the habit and you cannot put it aside, you are no more a master of yourself, then it is a sin. But its being a sin comes out of your unconsciousness, not out of the act itself.

No act is virtuous, no act is a sin. What consciousness is behind the act — everything depends on that.

You say: *I cannot drop the habit of chain-smoking.*

I am less interested in your chain-smoking; I am more interested in your habit. *Any* habit that becomes a force, a dominating force over you, is a sin. One should live more in freedom. One should be able to do things not according to habits but according to the situations.

Life is continuously changing — it is a flux — and habits are stagnant. The more you are surrounded by habits, the more you are closed to life. You are not open, you don't have windows. You don't have any communication with life; you go on repeating your habits. They don't fit; they are not the right response to the situation, to the moment. They are always lagging behind, they are always falling short. That's the failure of your life.

So remember: I am against all kinds of habits. Good or bad is not the point; there is no good habit as such, there is no bad habit as such. Habits are all bad because habit means something unconscious has become a dominating factor in your life, has become decisive. You are no more the deciding factor. The response is not coming out of awareness but out of a pattern, structure, that you have learned in the past.

Two members of the Shalom Retirement Home, Blustein and Levin, were strolling past the home of Nelson Rockefeller.

"If I only had that man's millions," sighed Blustein, "I would be richer than he is."

"Don't be a dummy," said Levin. "If you had his millions you would be as rich as he is, not any richer."

"You are wrong," said Blustein, "don't forget — I could give Hebrew lessons on the side!"

That's what he has been doing. Even if he becomes Nelson Rockefeller he will go on giving Hebrew lessons on the side. That's how people are living, just according to habits.

I have seen many rich people living very poor lives. Before they became rich their habits became settled — and their habits became settled when they were poor. That's why you find so much miserliness in rich people; it comes from the habits that became ingrained in them when they were poor.

One of the richest men in the world — not *one* of the richest but *the* richest man in the world it is thought — was the Nizam of Hyderabad. His collection of diamonds was the greatest in the world because he owned the diamond mines of Golconda which have provided the greatest diamonds to the world. The Kohinoor comes from Golconda. It was once in the Nizam's possession. He had so many diamonds that it is said that no one has ever been able to calculate exactly the price of his collection. Thousands and thousands of diamonds — they were not counted, they were weighed!

Try It My Way

But he was one of the most miserly men in the world. He used a single cap for thirty years. It was stinking but he wouldn't change it. He continued to wear the same coat for almost his whole life and he would not give it to be washed because they might destroy it. He was so miserly — you cannot imagine — that he would collect half-smoked cigarettes from the guests' ashtrays and then smoke them. The richest man in the world smoking cigarette butts smoked by others! The first thing he would do whenever a guest left was to search in the ashtrays and collect the ends of the cigarettes.

When he died, his greatest diamond was found in his dirty shoes. He was hiding it in his shoe! Maybe he had some idea behind it — that maybe he would be able to take it with him to the other world. Maybe he was afraid: "When I am dead, people may steal it." It was the greatest diamond; he used that diamond as a paper-weight on his table. Before he died he must have put it inside his shoe.

Even when one is dying one is moving in old habits, following old patterns.

I have heard:

The old Mulla Nasruddin had become a very rich man. When he felt death approaching he decided to make some arrangements for his funeral, so he ordered a beautiful coffin made of ebony wood with satin pillows inside. He also had a beautiful silk kaftan made for his dead body to be dressed in.

The day the tailor delivered the kaftan, Mulla Nasruddin tried it on to see how it would look, but suddenly he exclaimed, "What is this! Where are the pockets?"

Gurucharan, smoking or no smoking, that is not important. Maybe if you continue to smoke you will die a little earlier. So what? The world is so overpopulated, you will do some good by dying a little earlier. Maybe you will have tuberculosis. So what? Tuberculosis is now almost like the common cold. In fact, there is no cure for the common cold but there is a cure for tuberculosis. I know it because I suffer from a common cold. To have tuberculosis is to be very fortunate.

A man was suffering from a common cold for many years. All the doctors were tired of the man because nobody was able to cure him. Then a new doctor came to the town. All the other doctors told the new doctor, "Beware of this man! He is going to haunt you! He is a nuisance — his cold cannot be cured."

In fact, there is no cure for the common cold. They say that if you take medicine it goes within seven days; if you don't take the medicine it goes in one week.

So the new doctor was ready and the man appeared, as predicted by the others. The new doctor said, "I can cure it. You do one thing" — it must have been winter-time, just like this morning — he told him, "You do one thing: tomorrow, early in the morning, before sunrise, go to the lake; swim in the lake naked, then stand on the bank in the cold wind."

The man said, "Are you mad or something? How is that going to cure my common cold?"

The doctor said, "Who told you that it is going to cure your common cold? It will give you influenza, and I can cure that!"

So it is possible, Gurucharan, that you may die two years earlier, you may get tuberculosis — but it is not a sin. Don't be worried about *that*.

If you really want to do something about your life, dropping smoking is not going to help — because I know people who drop smoking; then they start chewing gum. The same old stupidity! Or if they are Indians they start chewing *paan;* it is the same. You will do something or other. Your unconsciousness will demand some activity, some occupation. It is an occupation. And it is only a symptom; it is not really the problem. It is not the root of the problem.

Have you not observed? Whenever you feel emotionally disturbed you immediately start smoking. It gives you a kind of relief; you become occupied. Your mind is distracted from the emotional problem. Whenever people feel tense they start smoking. The problem is tension, the problem is emotional disturbance — the problem is somewhere else; smoking is just an occupation. So you become engaged in taking the smoke in and out and you forget for the time being ... because mind cannot think of two things together, remember it. One of the fundamentals of mind is: it can think only of one thing at one time; it is one-dimensional. So if you are smoking and thinking of smoking, then from *all* other anxieties you are distracted.

That's the whole secret of the so-called spiritual mantras: they are nothing but distractions, like smoking. You repeat "Om, Om, Om," or "Ram, Ram, Ram," or "Allah, Allah, Allah" — that is just giving mind an occupation. And all these people who teach mantras say, "Repeat it as quickly as possible, so that between two repetitions there is not even a small gap. Let them overlap — so 'Ram Ram Ram' — don't leave a gap between two Rams, otherwise some thought may enter. Repeat like crazy!"

Yes, it will give you a certain relief — the same relief that comes from smoking, because your mind will be distracted from the anxieties and the world. You will forget about the world; you have created a trick. All mantras are tricks, but they are spiritual. Chain-smoking is also a mantra. It is a worldly mantra; non-religious you can call it, secular.

The real problem is the habit.

You say: *I have tried hard to drop it...*

You have not tried to be conscious of it; without trying to be conscious you have tried to drop it. It is not possible. It will come back, because your mind is the same; its needs are the same, its problems are the same, its anxieties, tensions are the same, its anguish is the same. And when those anxieties arise, what will you do? Immediately, mechanically, you will start searching for the cigarettes.

You may have decided again and again, and again and again you have failed — not because smoking is such a great phenomenon that you cannot get out of it, but because you are trying from the wrong end. Rather than becoming aware of the whole situation — why you smoke in the first place — rather than becoming aware of the process of smoking, you are simply trying to drop it. It is like pruning the leaves of a tree without cutting the roots.

And my whole concern here is to cut the roots, not to prune the tree. By pruning the leaves and the branches the tree will become thicker, the foliage will become thicker. You will not destroy the tree; you will be helping it, in fact. If you really want to get out of it you will have to look deeper, not into the symptoms but the roots. Where are the roots?

You must be a deeply anxiety-ridden person, otherwise chain-smoking is not possible; chain-smoking is a by-product. You must be so concerned about a thousand and one disturbances inside, you must be carrying such a big load of worries on your heart, on your chest, that you don't even know how to forget them. You don't know how to drop them — smoking at least helps you to forget about them.

You say: *I have tried hard...*

Now one thing has to be understood. The hypnotists have discovered a fundamental law; they call it the Law of

Try It My Way

Reverse Effect. If you try hard to do something without understanding the fundamentals, just the opposite will be the result.

It is like when you are learning how to ride on a bicycle. You are on a silent road, no traffic, early in the morning, and you see a red milestone just standing there by the side of the road like Hanuman. A sixty-foot-wide road and just a small milestone, and you become afraid: you may get to the milestone, you may hit against the milestone. Now you forget about the sixty-foot-wide road. In fact, even if you go blindfolded there is not much chance of your encountering the milestone, crashing into the milestone, but with open eyes now the whole road is forgotten; you have become focused. In the first place, that redness is very focusing. And you are so much afraid! — you want to avoid it. You have forgotten that you are on a bicycle; you have forgotten everything. Now the only problem for you is how to avoid this stone; otherwise you may harm yourself, you may crash into it.

Now the crash is absolutely inevitable; you are bound to crash with the stone. And then you will be surprised: "I tried hard." In fact, it is *because* you tried hard that you reached the stone. And the closer you come, the harder you try to avoid it; but the harder you try to avoid it, the more focused you become on it. It becomes a hypnotic force, it hypnotizes you. It becomes like a magnet.

It is a very fundamental law in life. Many people try avoiding many things and they fall into the same things. Try to avoid anything with great effort and you are bound to fall into the same pit. You cannot avoid it; that is not the way to avoid it.

Be relaxed. Don't try hard, because it is through relaxation that you can become aware, not by trying hard. Be calm, quiet, silent.

Try It My Way

I will suggest: smoke as much as you want to smoke. It is not a sin in the first place. I give you the guarantee — I will be responsible. I take the sin on myself, so if you meet God on Judgment Day you can just tell him that this fellow is responsible. And I will stand there as a witness for you that you are not responsible. So don't be worried about its being a sin. Relax and don't try to drop it with effort. No, that is not going to help.

Zen believes in effortless understanding.

So this is my suggestion: smoke as much as you want to smoke — just smoke meditatively. If Zen people can drink tea meditatively, why can't you smoke meditatively? In fact, tea contains the same stimulant as the cigarettes contain; it is the same stimulant, there is not much difference. Smoke meditatively, very religiously. Make it a ceremony. Try it *my* way.

Make a small corner in your house just for smoking: a small temple devoted, dedicated to the god of smoking. First bow down to your cigarette packet. Have a little chit-chat, talk to the cigarettes. Enquire, "How are you?" And then very slowly take a cigarette out — very slowly, as slowly as you can, because only if you take it very slowly will you be aware. Don't do it in a mechanical way, as you always do. Then tap the cigarette on the packet very slowly and for as long as you want. There is no hurry either. Then take the lighter, bow down to the lighter. These are great gods, deities! Light is God, so why not the lighter?

Then start smoking very slowly, just like *vipassana*. Don't do it like a *pranayama* — quick and fast and deep — but very slowly. Buddha says: Breathe naturally. So you smoke naturally: very slow, no hurry. If it is a sin you are in a hurry. If it is a sin you want to finish it as soon as possible. If it is a sin you don't want to look at it. You go

41

on reading the newspaper and you go on smoking. Who wants to look at a sin? But it is not a sin, so watch it — watch each of your acts.

Divide your acts into small fragments so you can move very slowly. And you will be surprised: by watching your smoking, slowly slowly smoking will become less and less. And one day suddenly...it is gone. You have not made any effort to drop it; it has dropped of its own accord, because by becoming aware of a dead pattern, a routine, a mechanical habit, you have created, you have released, a new energy of consciousness in you. Only that energy can help you; nothing else will ever help.

And it is not only so with smoking, Gurucharan, it is so with everything else in life: don't try too hard to change yourself. That leaves scars. Even if you change, your change will remain superficial. And you will find a substitute somewhere; you will *have* to find a substitute, otherwise you will feel empty.

And when something withers away of its own accord because you have become so silently aware of the stupidity of it that no effort is needed, when it simply falls, just like a dead leaf falling from a tree, it leaves no scar behind and it leaves no ego behind.

If you drop something by effort, it creates great ego. You start thinking, "Now I am a very virtuous man because I don't smoke." If you think that smoking is a sin, naturally, obviously, if you drop it you will think you are a very virtuous man.

That's how your virtuous men are. Somebody does not smoke, somebody does not drink, somebody eats only once a day, somebody does not eat in the night, somebody has even stopped drinking water in the night... and they are all great saints! These are saintly qualities, great virtues!

We have made religion so silly. It has lost all glory. It has become as stupid as people are. But the whole thing depends on your attitude: if you think something is a sin, then your virtue will be just the opposite of it.

I emphasize: not-smoking is not virtue, smoking is not sin; awareness is virtue, unawareness is sin. And then the same law is applicable to your whole life.

The third question
Osho,

The other day in discourse you said that sannyas only comes when the point of suicide has been reached. But I did not feel suicidal when I took sannyas, only in deep love with you. My life seemed rich, but you have made it infinitely richer. Am I not a true sannyasin because I don't feel suicidal?

Prem Sunderam,

AND WHAT IS LOVE? IT IS THE GREATEST SUICIDE IN THE WORLD! LOVE means committing suicide: the suicide of the ego. Love means dropping the ego. That's why people are so much afraid of love. They talk about it, they pretend also. They manage to befool others and themselves too that they love. But they avoid love — because love requires you first to die; only then are you resurrected.

Try It My Way

So what I said is absolutely true and absolutely applicable to you. And life certainly becomes richer. The more you die to the ego, the richer your life is, the more your life is full of overflowing love and joy and ecstasy.

No, you are my true sannyasin — but love is the ultimate in suicide. All other suicides are small suicides. Somebody commits suicide; that is only physical. Love is psychological suicide and meditation is spiritual suicide. In love you die psychologically, you drop the psychological ego, and in meditation you drop the very idea of the self, even of the supreme self. You become a nothingness...and in that nothingness blooms the white lotus of a Buddha.

The fourth question

Osho,

How can I learn the secrets of life?

Rabindra,

THERE ARE NO SECRETS IN LIFE. OR YOU CAN SAY: LIFE IS AN OPEN secret. Everything is available, nothing is hidden. All that you need is just eyes to see.

It is like a blind man asking: "I want to learn the secret of light." All that he needs is treatment of the eyes so that he can see. Light is available, it is not a secret. But he is blind — for him there is no light. What to say about light? For him there is not even darkness — because even to see darkness eyes are needed. A blind man cannot see darkness. If you can see darkness you can see light; they are two aspects of the same coin. The blind man knows nothing of darkness and nothing of light. Now he wants to learn the secrets of light.

We can only help him, not by teaching him great truths about light — they will be useless — but by operating on his eyes.

That's exactly what is being done here. This is an operation theater. The moment you become a sannyasin you are getting ready for the operation table, and you have to pass through many surgical operations. That's what all the therapies are. And if you survive all the therapies, then I am there finally to finish you off!

The moment the ego disappears, all the secrets are open secrets. Life is not like a fist; it is an open hand.

But people enjoy the idea that life has secrets — hidden secrets. Just to avoid their blindness they have created the idea of hidden secrets, of esoteric knowledge which is not available to anybody, or is available only to great adepts who live in Tibet or in the Himalayas, or who are no more in their bodies, who live only in astral bodies and appear only to a few chosen people. And all kinds of nonsense has been perpetuated down the ages for the simple reason that you want to avoid seeing, recognizing the simple fact of your blindness. Rather than saying, "I am blind," you say, "Life's secrets are very hidden; they are not easily available. You will need great initiation."

Life is not esoteric at all. It is written on each leaf of each tree, on each pebble on the seashore; it is contained in each ray of the sun — whatever you come across is life in all its beauty. And life is not afraid of you, so why should it hide itself? In fact, *you* are hiding, continuously trying to hide yourself. You are closing yourself against life because you are afraid of life. You are afraid to live — because life requires a constant death.

Try It My Way

One has to die every moment to the past. That is a great requirement of life — simple if you understand that the past is no more. Slip out of it, snap out of it! It is finished. Close the chapter, don't go on carrying it! And then life is available to you.

But you remain in the past; the past goes on hanging around you, the hangover never ends. And rather than coming to the present, the hangover of the past pushes you towards the future. So either you are in the memories or you are in your imagination. These are the two ways to miss life; otherwise there is no need to miss life. Just drop out of memories and out of imagination. Past is no more, future is not yet; both are non-existential. All that exists is the present, the now. Now is God.

Enter the doors of the now and all is revealed — instantly revealed, immediately revealed. Life is not a miser: it never hides anything, it does not hold anything back. It is ready to give all, totally and unconditionally. But *you* are not ready.

And Rabindra, you ask: *How can I learn the secrets of life?*

It is not a question of learning; it is more a question of unlearning. You have already learned too much: the Vedas, the Upanishads, the Gita, the Koran, the Bible, the Talmud. Thousands of scriptures are there inside you, clamoring, making noise, fighting with each other; all kinds of ideologies constantly trying to attract your attention. Your mind is a mess! It is overcrowded, it is a multitude. Unlearn! All that you have accumulated up to now as knowledge, unlearn it.

Zen people are right when they say: *Not knowing is the most intimate.*

Unlearning is the process that can bring you to that

beautiful space of not knowing. And then observe. Observe life without any knowledge interpreting it. You have become so accustomed to interpretation.

The moment you see the sunset, immediately, habitually, you repeat words that you have heard from others: "What a beautiful sunset!" You don't mean anything by it; you are not even looking at the sunset. You have not allowed it to penetrate to your heart. You are not feeling any wonder. You are not in a state of awe. You have not fallen on your knees. You are not looking with unblinking eyes, absorbing. Nothing of that. Just a casual remark: "What a beautiful sunset!" Just a way of speaking, a mannerism, showing that you are cultured, sophisticated, that you know what beauty is, that you have a great aesthetic sense, that you have great sensitivity towards nature. You are not looking at the sunset. Have you ever looked at the sunset? If you had looked you would not have asked this question; the sunset would have told you all.

Have you ever looked at a roseflower? Yes, you say, "It is beautiful!" You may repeat the famous saying: "A rose is a rose is a rose," but you are not seeing the rose. You are full of words, all kinds of jargon — poetic, philosophic — but between you and the roseflower there is such a wall, a China Wall. Behind that wall you are hiding.

And you are asking: *How can I learn the secrets of life?* And life goes on utterly nude, utterly naked, absolutely available. All that is required is a not-knowing state, an empty space which can absorb it, which can receive it. Only when you are in a state of not knowing are you a host, and then life becomes a guest.

Just observe with no evaluation. Don't say "good", don't say "bad"; don't say "beautiful", don't say "ugly". Don't say anything at all! Without saying anything, without bringing your mind in, just watch with utterly empty eyes, like a mirror. Reflect the moon, the stars, the sun, the trees, the people, the animals, the birds. And life will pour itself into your being. And it is an inexhaustible source of energy. And energy is delight.

William Blake is right when he says: Energy is delight. And when life pours its energy into your being it rejuvenates you, it revitalizes you; you are constantly reborn. A real, alive person is born again and again every *moment*. He is fresh, he is always young. Even when he dies he is fresh and young. Even in the moment of death, life is pouring more and more energy into him. His way of approaching life — without mind — helps him to see not only life but death too. And when you are able to see life, you are able to see death. And to see death means there is no death; all is life, and eternal, beginningless, endless. And you are part of this infinite celebration.

Just watch, be alert, and function from a state of innocence. Your question seems to be knowledgeable.

You say: *How can I learn the secrets of life?*
You are still asking like a student, a schoolboy.

Life is ready every moment to embrace you. *You* are hiding away from life because you are afraid. You want life on your terms. You want life to be Hindu or Mohammedan or Christian, and life cannot do that. You want life according to the Gita or the Koran, and life cannot do that.

Don't put conditions on life. Putting conditions on life is ugly, violent, stupid. Remain unconditionally open ... and suddenly some bells in your heart start ringing, in tune with the whole. A music arises, a melody is born. You are no more separate as a learner, as a knower. Finally you are not even separate as an observer; the observer and the observed become one ultimately.

Try It My Way

That is the moment of enlightenment, of Buddhahood, when you are part of this whole, an intrinsic part, inseparable. Then you *are* life — what is the need to learn anything? You *are* it; you are not separate from it. Who is going to learn and about what? You are life. Then experiencing arises: not knowing but experiencing, not knowledge but wisdom.

Raul was sitting against the wall of his friend Pablo's adobe shack. Pablo came out of the house with a butterfly in his hand.

"Ay, Pablo," called Raul. "Where are you going with the butterfly?"

"I am going to get some butter," replied Pablo.

"Oh, you foolish fellow!" said Raul. "You cannot get butter with a butterfly!"

A few minutes later, to Raul's astonishment, Pablo returned with a bucket of butter.

In a little while Pablo came out, this time carrying a jar of horseflies.

"Ay, Pablo," called Raul, "where are you going with them horseflies?"

"Where you think?" answered Pablo. "To get horses, of course!"

Pablo returned in a few minutes leading a pair of beautiful stallions.

"See, I told you!" said Pablo to the amazed Raul.

Ten minutes later Pablo came out clutching a handful of pussy willows.

"Ay, Pablo!" shouted Raul. "Wait for me — I go with you!"

Just observe. Nothing is hidden — just observe. And slowly slowly you will start going with life. Slowly slowly you will not remain separate, you will follow life. And to follow life is to be religious. Not to follow Christ, not to follow Buddha, but to follow life is to be religious.

The fifth question
Osho,

I can find the answer to all the questions I ask you within myself, but still I would like to ask you one — just for fun, simply taking up your invitation. Is it really possible for an ordinary person like myself to live in this world, earning and spending, and still be in the state of no-mind constantly?

Deva David,

I WILL NOT ANSWER THIS QUESTION — JUST FOR FUN! IF YOU CAN FIND the answer to all the questions, find out the answer to this one too!

And you don't seem to be an *ordinary* person — one who can find all the answers to all the questions within himself can't be an ordinary person, otherwise how will you define the extraordinary?

No, I will not bother you with an answer — you find it within yourself. When you cannot find it, then ask me again.

Try It My Way

The sixth question

Osho,

Can't one believe in God without seeing him?

Surendra Mohan,

WHO IS TELLING YOU TO BELIEVE IN GOD? I AM AGAINST ALL BELIEF. You must be a very newcomer here. Belief is irreligious, as much as disbelief is. Belief means you don't know yet you have accepted something. It is cowardly — you have not enquired. You are pretending, you are a hypocrite.

All believers are hypocrites — Catholic and communist, Jainas and Jews — all. Believers are hypocrites. They don't know and yet they pretend *as if* they know. What is belief? It is playing the game of "as if". And the same is true about disbelief.

The communist knows *not* that there is no God, just as the Hindu knows not that there is a God. The Hindu believes there is a God, the communist believes there is no God. Disbelief is also a kind of belief — a negative kind of belief. And that's why it is so easy to become a Hindu from being a communist or a communist from being a Hindu.

It is a well-known fact that before the Russian revolution Russia was one of the *most* religious countries in the world. Then what happened? After ten years of revolution, the whole country became atheistic. The same people who were fanatical believers became fanatical *dis*believers! On the surface it looks puzzling, but it is not. The fanaticism is the same; nothing has changed. They were fanatic Christians, now they are fanatic communists. They believed madly, now they disbelieve madly, their madness is the same. And their belief was wrong because they had not experienced it, and their disbelief is wrong because they have not yet experienced the *absence* of God.

Surendra Mohan, you ask me: *Can't one believe in God without seeing him?*
In the first place there is no need to believe in God. And if you believe you will never be able to know him. Belief will become a barrier; belief is always a barrier. Belief means you are carrying a prejudice, and you will not be able to see that which is. You will project your own idea.

That's why a Hindu, when he comes to a vision of God, will see Krishna with the flute. He will never see Christ, he will never see Mahavira, he will never see Buddha. And the Christian? He has never seen Krishna or Buddha. And a Jew? He has his own ideas. So when you see, what you see is not really the real but your own projection, your own idea.

Remember: as long as you have even a single idea inside you, your experience is going to be distorted by it.

My suggestion to *my* people is: don't carry any idea of God, for or against. Don't carry any image of God. In fact, God is absolutely irrelevant — be meditative! And meditation means: drop all thoughts, drop all ideologies, drop all knowledge. Drop the mind itself.

And then when you are in a state of no-mind, something unimaginable, unbelievable, unpredictable, inexpressible, is experienced. You can call it God, you can call it truth, you can call it *nirvana,* or whatsoever you want to call it. You are free because no word describes it, hence any word is as good as any other. But don't carry any belief.

And what do you mean: "...without seeing him"? Do

you think someday you will see God? Is God a person? That's how people think: God is like Rama, always carrying a bow with arrows. Now, in the twentieth century, carrying a bow would look so foolish. Give him an atom bomb — that will look far more contemporary! Jesus on the cross ... twenty centuries have passed. Now we have electric chairs! Give him an electric chair. At least he can rest on the chair! Still you go on giving him a cross. Make your ideas a little more contemporary. They are all out of date.

What do you mean by "*seeing* God"? Is he a person? Will you say hello and will you shake hands with him? God is not a person, hence God cannot be seen in that sense. God is a presence.

There is no God but godliness. It is a quality, a fragrance. You experience it, you don't see it. And when you experience it, it is not something out there as an object; it is something *in here*, in the heart of your hearts. It is your subjectivity, it is your consciousness.

So there is no question of belief and there is no question of seeing either.

But people are brought up in all kinds of beliefs and they go on seeing through their prejudices. So anything that fits with their prejudices enters inside; anything that does not fit with their prejudice is prevented from entering.

An elephant escaped from the local zoo and made his way into the vegetable garden of one of the town's most prominent matrons. Unfortunately this lady had only just returned from a cocktail party where she had had just a little too much to drink. She was not too drunk, however, to see the beast in her garden, and she had the presence of mind to call the police.

"Quick," she said, "there is some kind of huge, strange looking animal in my garden."

Try It My Way

"What is he doing?" asked the desk sergeant.

"He seems to be picking lettuce with his tail!"

"Oh, really?" replied the wary policeman. "And what is he doing with it?"

The lady peered out into her garden once more and then said, "Sergeant, even if I told you, you would never believe it!"

God has been experienced. Nobody has ever been able to say exactly what that experience is. And even if somebody tries to say it, you are not going to believe it. Your prejudices, your *a priori* ideas, will prevent you.

No, Surendra Mohan, no need to believe in God; no need even to believe that one day you are going to see him. In fact, God is not a religious subject at all — you will be surprised when you hear it — God is a philosophic subject. It is for those useless people who go on endlessly into logic-chopping and hair-splitting. It is for those people to discuss God.

A religious person is not interested in God; he is more interested in the very source of his being, who he is: "Who am I?" That is the *most* fundamental religious question — not God, not heaven, not hell, but "Who am I?" And if you can find the truth of your own being you will have found all the truth that is necessary to know and is worth knowing. You will have found God and you will have found *nirvana* and you will have found all that the seers, the *rishis*, the Buddhas, the prophets, down the ages, have been telling you to enquire into.

But don't make a philosophical enquiry, otherwise you will end up with a conclusion. And all conclusions are dangerous because once you conclude you become fanatical about your conclusion, you start clinging to it. You become afraid of truth — because who knows truth may disturb

Try It My Way

your conclusion, and your conclusion is so cozy and so convenient, and it has helped to give you a certain feeling of security? So you go on clinging to your conclusion — and your conclusion is your conclusion.

If you are unaware, what value can your conclusion have? Your conclusion cannot be bigger than you, your conclusion cannot be higher than you. Your conclusion will be as high, as deep, as you are high and you are deep. Your conclusion will only reflect you.

God is not a conclusion. It is not arrived at by logical processes — by believing, by discussing, by analyzing, no. All mind processes have to cease. When all processes have ceased, something — call it XYZ — suddenly wells up within you. A few qualities can be indicated: you will feel tremendously ecstatic, blissful, at home, at ease. For the first time existence will be your home. You will not be an outsider, a stranger. For the first time there will be no conflict between you and existence, no struggle for the survival of the fittest. For the first time you will be in a state of let-go. And in let-go wells up great joy.

You will be able to sing the song that you have brought in your heart and is still unsung. You will be able to bloom into thousands of flowers. Or as in the East we say: you will bloom into a thousand-petalled lotus of consciousness, of awareness. That is God — or better, godliness.

Try It My Way

The seventh question
Osho,

I know you are against marriage, but I still want to get married. Can I have your blessings?

Rakesh,

MEDITATE OVER MURPHY'S MAXIM: A FOOL AND HIS COOL ARE SOON parted.

It is not yet published anywhere, but Asha is the custodian of Murphy's unpublished manuscripts, so she goes on supplying these maxims of Murphy to me. Meditate over it: A fool and his cool are soon parted.

That's what marriage is going to be. Only fools think in terms of legality; otherwise, love is enough. And I am not against marriage — I am for love. If love becomes your marriage, good; but don't hope that marriage can bring love. That is not possible. Love can become a marriage. You have to work very consciously to transform your love into a marriage.

Ordinarily, people destroy their love. They do *everything* to destroy it and then they suffer. And they go on saying, "What went wrong?" They destroy — they do everything to destroy it.

There is a tremendous desire and longing for love, but love needs great awareness. Only then can it reach its highest climax — and that highest climax *is* marriage. It has nothing to do with law. It is a merging of two hearts into totality. It is the functioning of two persons in synchronicity — that is marriage.

But people try love and because they are unconscious ... their longing is good, but their love is full of jealousy, full of possessiveness, full of anger, full of nastiness. Soon they destroy it. Hence for centuries they have depended on marriage. Better to start by marriage so that the law can protect you from destroying it. The society, the government, the court, the policeman, the priest, they will all force you to live in the institution of marriage, and you will be just a slave. If marriage is an institution, you are going to be a slave in it. Only slaves want to live in institutions.

Marriage is a totally different phenomenon: it is the climax of love. Then it is good. I am not against marriage — I am for the *real* marriage. I am against the false, the pseudo, that exists. But it is an arrangement. It gives you a certain security, safety, occupation. It keeps you engaged. Otherwise, it gives you no enrichment, it gives you no nourishment.

So, Rakesh, if you want to get married according to me, only then can I give you my blessings.

Learn to love, and drop all that goes against love. It is an uphill task. It is the greatest art in existence, to be able to love. One needs such refinement, such inner culture, such meditativeness, so that one can see immediately how one goes on destroying. If you can avoid being destructive, if you become creative in your relationship; if you support it, nourish it; if you are capable of compassion for the other person, not only passion.... Passion alone is not able to sustain love; compassion is needed. If you are able to be compassionate towards the other; if you are able to accept his limitations, his imperfections; if you are able to accept him the way he is or she is and *still* love — then one day a marriage happens. That may take years. That may take your whole life.

Try It My Way

You can have my blessings, but for a legal marriage you need not have my blessings — and my blessings won't be of any help either. And beware! Before you jump into it, give it a second thought.

A woman walks into a pet shop and sees a bird with a big beak. "What is that strange looking bird?" she asks the proprietor.

"That is a gobble bird," he answers.

"Why do you call him a gobble bird?"

The man says to the bird, "Gobble bird, my chair!"

The bird immediately starts pecking away and gobbles up the chair.

"I will buy him," the woman says.

The owner asks why.

"Well," she says, "when my husband comes home he will see the bird and ask, 'What is that?' I will say, 'A gobble bird.' And then he will say, 'Gobble bird, my foot!'"

Just be a little aware before you move! My blessings won't help. Marriage is a trap and your wife sooner or later will find a gobble bird.

Mrs. Moskowitz loved chicken soup. One evening she was spooning it up when three of her husband's friends came in. "Mrs. Moskowitz," the spokesman said, "we are here to tell you that your husband, Izzy, has been killed in an automobile accident."

Mrs. Moskowitz continued eating her soup. Again they told her. Still no reaction.

"Look," said the puzzled speaker, "we are telling you that your husband is dead!"

She went right on with the soup. "Gentlemen," she said between mouthfuls, "soon as I am finished with this chicken soup, you gonna hear some scream!"

Marriage is not love; it is something else.

Try It My Way

A woman at the grave of her husband was wailing, "Oh, Joseph, it is four years since you have gone, but I still miss you!"

Just then Grossberg passed by and saw the woman crying. "Excuse me," he said, "who are you mourning?"

"My husband," she said. "I miss him so much!"

Grossberg looked at the stone and then said, "Your husband? But it says on the gravestone 'Sacred to the memory of Golda Kreps'."

"Oh, yes, he put everything in my name."

So be a little aware before you are trapped! Marriage is a trap: you will be trapped by the woman and the woman will be trapped by you. It is a mutual trap. And then legally you are allowed to torture each other forever. And particularly in this country, not only for one life but for lives together! Divorce is not even allowed after you are dead. Next life also you will get the same wife, remember!

And the last question
Osho,

What is going on?

Anand Subhuti,

I AM SURPRISED, BECAUSE THAT'S EXACTLY WHAT I WAS GOING TO ASK you all! I don't know. But: *Not knowing is the most intimate.*

The ancients said:

"(Self-)cultivation takes an unimaginable time (while) enlightenment in an instant is attained."

If the training is efficient, enlightenment will be attained in one fingersnap.

In days gone by Ch'an Master Hui Chueh of Lang Yeh mountain, had a disciple who called on him for instruction. The Master taught her to examine into the sentence: "Take no notice."

She followed his instruction strictly without backsliding.

One day her house caught fire, but she said: "Take no notice."

Another day, her son fell into the water and when a bystander called her, she said: "Take no notice."

She observed exactly her Master's instruction by laying down all casual thoughts.

One day, as her husband lit the fire to make fritters of twisted dough, she threw into the pan full of boiling (vegetable) oil a batter which made a noise.

Upon hearing the noise, she was instantly enlightened. Then she threw the pan of oil on the ground, clapped her hands and laughed.

Thinking she was insane, her husband scolded her and said: "Why do you do this? Are you mad?"

She replied: "Take no notice."

Then she went to the Master Hui Chueh and asked him to verify her achievement.

The Master confirmed that she had obtained the holy fruit.

Take No Notice

THERE ARE TWO PATHS TO THE ULTIMATE TRUTH. THE FIRST IS OF SELF-cultivation and the second is of enlightenment. The first is basically wrong. It only appears to be a path; it is not. One goes on and on in circles, but one never arrives. The second does not appear to be a path because there is no space for a path when something happens instantly, when something happens immediately. When something happens without taking any time, how can there be a path?

This paradox has to be understood as deeply as possible: the first appears to be the path but is not; the second appears not to be a path but is. The first appears to be a path because there is infinite time; it is a time phenomenon. But anything happening in time cannot lead you beyond time; anything happening in time only strengthens time.

Time means mind. Time *is* a projection of mind. It does not exist; it is only an illusion. Only the present exists — and the present is not part of time. The present is part of eternity. Past is time, future is time; both are non-existential. The past is only memory and the future is only imagination; memory and imagination, both are non-existential. We create the past because we cling to memory; clinging to the memory is the source of the past. And we create the future because we have so many desires yet to be fulfilled, we have so many imaginations yet to be realized. And desires need a future like a screen onto which they can be projected.

Past and future are mind phenomena; and past and future make your whole idea of time. Ordinarily you think that time is divided into three divisions: past, present and future. That is totally wrong. That is not how the awakened ones have seen time. They say time consists only of two divisions: past and future. The present is not part of time at all; the present belongs to the beyond.

The first path — the path of self-cultivation — is a time path; it has nothing to do with eternity. And truth is eternity.

The second path — the path of enlightenment, Zen Masters have always called the pathless path because it does not appear to be a path at all. It cannot appear as a path, but just for the purposes of communication we will call it "the second path," arbitrarily. The second path is not part of time, it is part of eternity. Hence it happens instantaneously; it happens in the present. You cannot desire it, you cannot be ambitious for it.

On the first path, the false path, all is allowed. You can imagine, you can desire, you can be ambitious. You can change all your worldly desires into other-worldly desires. That's what the so-called religious people go on doing. They don't desire money any more — they are fed up with it, tired of it, frustrated with it, bored with it — but they start desiring God. Desire persists; it changes its object. Money is no more the object of desire but God; pleasure is no more the object of desire but bliss. But what bliss can you imagine? Whatsoever you imagine in the name of bliss is nothing but your idea of pleasure — maybe a little bit refined, cultivated, sophisticated, but it can't be more than that.

The people who stop desiring worldly things start desiring heaven and heavenly pleasures. But what are they? — magnified forms of the same old desires, in fact more dangerous than the worldly desires, because with the worldly desires one thing is absolutely certain: you are bound to get frustrated sooner or later. You will get out of them; you cannot remain in them forever. The very nature of them is such that they promise you, but they never fulfill their promises — the goods are never delivered. How long can you remain deceived by them? Even the *most* stupid person has glimpses, once in a while, that he is chasing illusions which cannot be fulfilled by the very nature of existence. The intelligent one comes to the realization sooner.

But with the other-worldly desires there is far greater danger because they are other-worldly, and to see them and to experience them you will have to wait till death. They will happen only after death so you cannot be free of them in life, while you are alive. And a man who has lived unconsciously his whole life, his death is going to be the culmination of unconsciousness; he will die in unconsciousness. In death also he will not be able to disillusion himself. And the person who dies in unconsciousness is born again in unconsciousness. It is a vicious circle; it goes on and on. And the person who is born in unconsciousness will repeat the same stupidities that he has been repeating for millions of lives.

Unless you become alert and aware *in* life, unless you change the quality of your living, you will not die consciously. And only a conscious death can bring you to a conscious birth; and then a far more conscious life opens its doors.

Changing worldly desires into other-worldly desires is the last strategy of the mind to keep you captive, to keep you a prisoner, to keep you in bondage.

Try It My Way

So the first path is not really a path but a deception — but a very alluring deception. In the first place, it is *self-cultivation*. It is not against the ego; it is rooted in the refinement of the ego. Refine your ego of all grossness, then you become a self. The ego is like a raw diamond: you go on cutting it and polishing it and then it becomes a Kohinoor, very precious. That is your idea of "self," but it is nothing but ego with a beautiful name, with a spiritual flavor thrown in. It is the same old illusory ego.

The very idea that "I am" is wrong. The whole is, God is — I am not. Either I can exist or God can exist; we cannot both exist together — because if *I* exist, then I am a separate entity. Then I have my own existence independent of God. But God simply means the total, the whole. How can I be independent of it? How can I be separate from it? If I exist, I destroy the very idea of totality.

The people who deny God are the most egoistic people. It is not an accident that Friedrich Nietzsche declared God dead. He was one of the most egoistic persons possible. It was his ego that made him insane finally. Ego is insanity, the basic insanity, the most fundamental, out of which all other insanities arise. He said: "God is dead and man is free." That sentence is significant. In one sentence he has said the whole thing: Man can be free only if God is dead; if God is alive, then man cannot be free, in fact man cannot exist.

The very idea that "I am" is unspiritual. The idea of the self is unspiritual.

And what is self-cultivation? It is an effort to polish; it is an effort to create a beautiful character, to drop all that is unrespectable and to create all that is respectable. That's why in different countries different things are cultivated by the spiritual people — the so-called spiritual. It depends on the society; what the society respects, that will be cultivated.

In Soviet Russia, before the revolution, there was a Christian sect which believed that sexual organs should be cut, only then are you real Christians. The statement of Jesus was taken literally. Jesus has said: Be eunuchs of God. And these fools followed it literally. Every year they would gather in thousands and in a mad frenzy they would cut their sexual organs. Men would cut their genital organs, women would cut their breasts. And those who were able to do it were thought to be saints; they were very much respected — they had made a great sacrifice. Now, anywhere else they would have been thought utterly insane; but because in that particular society it was respected, they were saints.

In India you can find many people lying down on beds of thorns or needles, and they are thought to be great sages. If you look into their eyes, they are just stupid people. Lying down on a bed of thorns can't make one spiritual. It will simply deaden your body, your sensitivity. Your body will become more and more dull; it will not feel.

That's how it happens. Your face does not feel the cold because it remains open; it becomes insensitive to the cold. Your hands don't feel the cold so much because they are open; they become insensitive to the cold. Exactly in the same way you can live naked. Only for the beginning few months will you feel the cold; slowly slowly your body will adjust.

That's how the Jaina monks live naked. And their followers praise them like anything; they think: "This is what real spirituality is. Look, they have gone beyond the body!" They have gone nowhere; the body has just become dull. And when the body becomes dull it naturally creates a

Try It My Way

dullness of the mind too, because body and mind are deeply one. The body is the outer shell of the mind and the mind is the inner core of the body.

If you really want to be a sensitive, intelligent mind, you need a sensitive, intelligent body too. Yes, the body has its own intelligence. Don't kill it, don't destroy it, otherwise you will be destroying your intelligence. But if it is respected, then it becomes something religious, spiritual, holy.

Anything that the society respects becomes a nourishment for your ego. And people are ready to do any stupid thing. The only joy is that it will bring respectability.

Self-cultivation is nothing but another name for ego-cultivation. It is not a real path. In fact, no real path is needed. It looks like a long long, arduous path; it needs many lives. The people who have been preaching self-cultivation know perfectly well that one life is not enough; otherwise they will be exposed. So they imagine many many lives, a long, arduous journey of many lives. Then finally, after an unimaginable time, you arrive. In fact, you never arrive. You cannot arrive because you are already there. Hence this very idea of a path leading to a goal is meaningless.

Try to understand the paradox; it is very significant in understanding the spirit of Zen.

ZEN IS NOT A WAY, IS NOT A PATH. HENCE THEY CALL IT THE GATELESS gate, the pathless path, the effortless effort, the actionless action. They use these contradictory terms just to point towards a certain truth: that a path means there is a goal

Take No Notice

and the goal has to be in the future. You are here, the goal is there, and between you and the goal a path is needed, a bridge, to join you. The very idea of a path means you have yet to arrive home, that you are not at home already.

The second path — the pathless path, the path of enlightenment — has a totally different revelation to make, a totally different declaration of immense value: that you are already it. *"Ah, this!"* There is nowhere to go, no need to go. There is *no one* to go. We are already enlightened. Then only can it happen in an instant — because it is a question of awakening.

For example, if you have fallen asleep and you are dreaming ... you can dream that you are on the moon. Do you think that if somebody wakes you up you will have to come back from the moon? Then it will take time. If you have already reached the moon, then you will have to come back and it will take time. The airship may not be available right now. There may be no tickets available; it may be full. But you can be awakened because it is only a dream that you are on the moon. In fact you are in your bed, in your home; you had not gone anywhere. Just a little shaking and you are suddenly back — back from your dreams.

The world is only a dream. We need not go anywhere; we have always been here; we *are* here and we are going to be here. But we can fall asleep and we can dream.

The All-Indian National Guard was out on maneuvers. They were about to begin a mock battle between the "red" team and the "blue" team when they received a telegram from Delhi: "Because of recent budget cuts we cannot supply weapons or ammunition, but please continue with your battle for training purposes."

The General called his troops together and said, "We will simulate the battle. If you are within a hundred yards of

Try It My Way

the enemy, point your arm and shout 'BANG-BANG' for a rifle. If you are within fifty feet, throw your arms over your head and shout 'BOOM' for a hand grenade. If you are within five feet, wave your arms and shout 'SLASH-SLASH' for a bayonet."

Private Abul was put on scout patrol, and apparently all the action went in another direction. He was out for three days and three nights, but did not see another person.

On the fourth day Abul was sitting under a tree, discouraged, when he saw a figure coming across the hill in his direction. He got down on his hands and knees and crawled through the mud and weeds, as he had been trained. Sure enough, it was a soldier from the other team.

Abul raised his arm and shouted "BANG-BANG!" but he got no response. So he ran up closer, threw his arm over his head, and shouted "BOOM!" very loudly. The other soldier did not even turn in his direction. So he ran right up to the soldier and shouted in his ear "SLASH-SLASH! SLASH-SLASH!" but still he got no reaction.

Abul was angry. He grabbed the other soldier by the arm and shouted, "Hey! You are not playing according to the rules. I went 'BANG-BANG,' I shouted 'BOOM,' and I came right up to you and said 'SLASH-SLASH,' and you have not even indicated that you have seen me yet."

At this point, the other soldier wheeled around to Abul and said in a deep voice, "RUMBLE-RUMBLE, I am a tank!"

This is the situation. You are not what you think you are, you are not what you believe you are. All your beliefs are dreams. Maybe you have been dreaming for so long that they appear almost like realities.

So the question is not of self-cultivation: the question is of enlightenment.

Zen believes in sudden enlightenment because Zen believes that you are already enlightened; just a certain situation is needed which can wake you up. Just a little alarm may do the work. If you are a little alert, just a little alarm and you are suddenly awake. And all the dream with all its long long desires, journeys, kingdoms, mountains, oceans ... they have all disappeared in a single instant.

This beautiful story:

> *The ancients said:*
>
> *"(Self-)cultivation takes an unimaginable time...."*

It is bound to take an unimaginable time because you will be fighting with shadows. You cannot conquer them, you cannot destroy them either. In fact, the more you fight with them, the more you believe in their existence. If you fight with your own shadow, do you think there is any possibility of your ever becoming victorious? It's impossible. And it is not because the shadow is stronger than you that the victory is impossible. Just the contrary: the shadow has *no* power, it has *no* existence, and you start fighting with something which is non-existential—how can you win? You will be dissipating your energy. You will become tired and the shadow will remain unaffected. It will not get tired. You cannot kill it, you cannot burn it, you cannot even escape from it. The faster you run, the faster it comes behind you.

The only way to get rid of it is to *see* that it is not there at all. Seeing that a shadow is a shadow is liberation. Just seeing, no cultivation! And once the shadows disappear, your life has a luminosity of its own. Certainly there will arise great perfume, but it will not be something cultivated; it will not be something painted from the outside.

That's the difference between a saint and a sage. A saint follows the path of self-cultivation. He practices non-violence, like Mahatma Gandhi; he practices truth, truthfulness; he practices sincerity, honesty. But these are all practices. And whenever you are practicing non-violence, what are you doing? What is really happening inside you? You must be repressing violence. When you are practicing — when you *have* to practice — truth, what does it mean? It simply means untruth arises in you and you repress it and you go against it, and you say the truth. But the untruth has not disappeared from your being. You can push it downwards into the very basement of your being; you can throw it into the deep darkness of the unconscious. You can become completely oblivious of it. You can forget that it exists, but it exists and it is bound to function from those deep, dark depths of your being in such a subtle way that you will never be aware that you are still in its grip — in fact, far more so than before because when it was consciously felt you were not so much in its grip. Now the enemy has become hidden.

That's my observation of Mahatma Gandhi. He observed, cultivated non-violence; but I have looked deeply into his life and he is one of the most violent men this century has known. But his violence is very polished; his violence is so sophisticated that it looks almost like non-violence. And his violence has such subtle ways that you cannot detect it easily. It comes from the back door; it is never at the front door. You will not find it in his drawing-room; it is not there. It has started living somewhere in the servants' quarters at the back of the house where nobody ever goes, but it goes on pulling his strings from there.

For example, if ordinarily you are angry, you are angry with the person who has provoked it. Mahatma Gandhi would be angry with himself, not with the person. He would turn his anger upon himself; he would make it introverted.

Take No Notice

Now it is very difficult to detect it. He would go on a fast, he would become suicidal, he would start torturing himself. And in a subtle way he would torture the other by torturing himself.

In his ashram, if somebody was found drinking tea.... Now tea is so innocent, but it was a sin in Mahatma Gandhi's ashram. These ashrams exist by creating guilt in people; they don't miss any opportunity to create guilt. That is their trade-secret, so no opportunity has to be missed. Even tea is enough; it has to be used. If somebody is found drinking tea, he is a sinner. He is committing a crime — far more than a crime, because a sin is something far deeper than a crime. If somebody was found...

And people used to drink tea. They would drink tea in hiding; they had to hide. Just to drink tea they had to be thieves, deceivers, hypocrites! That's what your so-called religions have done to millions of people. Rather than making them spiritual they have simply made them, reduced them to hypocrites.

They would pretend that they didn't drink tea, but once in a while they would be found red-handed. And Gandhi was searching, looking; he had agents planted to find out who was going against the rules. And whenever somebody was found he would be called ... and Gandhi would go on a fast to punish himself.

"What kind of logic is this?" you will ask. It is a very simple logic. In India it has been followed for centuries. The trick is that Gandhi used to say, "I must not yet be a perfect Master, that's why a disciple can deceive me. So I must purify myself. You could deceive me because I am not yet perfect. If I was perfect nobody could deceive me. How can you imagine deceiving a perfect Master? So there is some imperfection in me."

Try It My Way

Look at the humbleness! And he would torture himself; he would go on a fast. Now Gandhi is fasting because you have taken a cup of tea. How will *you* feel? His three days' fast for you, just for a single cup of tea! It will be too heavy on you. If he had hit you on the head it would not have been so heavy. If he had insulted you, punished you, told you to go on a fast for three days, it would have been far simpler — and far more compassionate. But the old man himself is fasting, torturing himself, and you are condemned by every eye in the ashram. Everybody is looking at you as a great sinner: "It is because of *you* that the Master is suffering. And just for a cup of tea? How low you have fallen!"

And the person would go and touch his feet and cry and weep, but Gandhi wouldn't listen. He had to purify himself.

This is all violence; I don't call it non-violence. It is violence with a vengeance, but in such a subtle way that it is very difficult to detect. Even Gandhi may not have been aware at all of what he was doing — because he was not practicing awareness, he was practicing non-violence.

You can go on practicing ... then there are a thousand and one things to be practiced. And when will you be able to get out of all that is wrong in your life? It will take an unimaginable time. And then, too, do you think you will be out of it? It is not possible; you will not be out of it.

I have never seen anybody arriving at truth by self-cultivation. In fact, the people who go for self-cultivation are not very intelligent people because they have missed the most fundamental insight: that we are not going anywhere, that God is not something to be achieved; God is already the *case* in you. You are pregnant with God, you are made of the stuff called God. Nothing has to be achieved — only a certain awareness, a *self*-awareness.

Take No Notice

There is an unusual store in New York where one can buy exotic foods from all over the world.

Mulla Nasruddin visited this store recently. He found rare tropical fruits from the jungles of South America and many strange delicacies from Africa and the Middle East.

In one corner he found a counter with several trays of human brains. There were politicians' brains at $1 per pound, engineers' brains at $2 per pound, and there was one tray of saints' brains at $50 per pound.

Since all the brains looked very much alike, he asked the man behind the counter, "Why do you charge so much more for the saints' brains?"

The man peered out from behind his glasses and answered, "Do you have any idea how many saints we have to go through to get a pound of brains?"

My observation of your so-called saints is exactly the same. I don't think they are very intelligent people — basically stupid, because unless one is stupid one cannot follow the path of self-cultivation. It *appears* only as a path; it is not. And it is tedious and it is long; in fact, it is unending.

You can change one habit; it will start asserting itself in something else. You can close one door and another door immediately opens. By the time you close that door a third door is bound to open — because basically you remain the same, the same old unconscious person. Trying to be humble you will be simply becoming more and more egoistic and nothing else. Your humbleness will be simply a new way of fulfilling your ego. Deep down you will imagine yourself to be the humblest person in the world — there is nobody who is more humble than you. Now, this is ego speaking a new language, but the meaning is the same. The language is changed but the meaning is the same; translated into a different language it does not change. First you were the greatest man in the world, now you are the humblest man in the world, but you remain special, you remain extraordinary, you remain superior. First you were this, now you are that, but deep down nothing has changed. Nothing can ever change by self-cultivation.

A man spent thousands of dollars going from doctor to doctor trying to find a cure for his insomnia. Finally a doctor was able to help him.

"You must be terribly relieved," said one of his friends sympathetically.

"You said it!" replied the former insomniac. "Why, sometimes I lie awake all night thinking of how I used to suffer."

So what has changed? Self-cultivation only gives you a deception: the deception that something is happening, that you are doing something, that something great is on the way; that if not today, tomorrow it is going to happen.

Hornstein manufactured coats, but business was so bad the poor man could not sleep.

"Count sheep," advised Slodnick, his friend. "It is the best-known cure."

"What can I lose?" said Hornstein. "I will try tonight."

The next morning he looked more bleary-eyed than ever.

"What happened?" asked Slodnick.

"Sheep I could count," moaned Hornstein. "I counted up to fifty thousand. Then I sheared the sheep and made up fifty thousand overcoats. Then came the problem that kept me awake all the rest of the night: where could I get fifty thousand linings?"

No such things are going to help because if the *mind* is the same, it will go on creating the same problem in different ways. Basically the roots have to be transformed; just pruning the leaves is not going to help. And self-cultivation is only pruning of the leaves.

The ancients said:

"(Self-)cultivation takes an unimaginable time (while) enlightenment in an instant is attained."

ENLIGHTENMENT IS ATTAINED IN A SINGLE MOMENT. WHY? — BECAUSE you are already enlightened. You have simply forgotten it. You have to be reminded, that's all.

The function of the Master is to remind you, not to give you a path but to give you a remembrance; not to give you methods of cultivation, not to give you a character, virtue, but only awareness, intelligence, awakening.

In a single moment it can be attained because you have never lost it in the first place. You are dreaming that you are unenlightened. You can dream you are in heaven, you can dream you are in hell. And you know! — you dream sometimes you are in heaven and sometimes in hell. In the morning you can be in heaven and by the evening you can be in hell. One moment you can be in heaven, another moment you can be in hell. It all depends on you. It is something to do with your psyche; it is not something outside you.

A man died, arrived at the Pearly Gates, and was shown by St. Peter to a waiting room. He sat there, naturally anxious to know whether he would be sent to Heaven or to Hell. The door opened and a famous saint walked in.

The man rejoiced, "I must be in Heaven!"

Just then the door opened again and a famous prostitute walked in. The man was confused. "In that case I must be in Hell!" he thought.

While he was still wondering, the saint grabbed the prostitute and started making love to her. The man, flabbergasted, ran to St. Peter and asked, "You *must* tell me: is this Heaven or Hell?"

"Can't you see?" answered St. Peter. "It is Heaven for him and Hell for her!"

Heaven and hell are not geographical; they are not something outside you, they are something that belongs to your interiority. If you are awake, then you are in a totally different universe; it is as if in your awakening the whole existence becomes awakened. It takes a new color, a new flavor, a new fragrance. When you are asleep, the whole existence sleeps with you. It *all* depends on you.

So the question is not of cultivating any character, of becoming virtuous, of becoming a saint. The question is how to come out of dreams, how to come out of the past and the future, how to be just herenow.

That's what enlightenment is... *"Ah, this!"*

When Alice was at the Mad Hatter's tea party, she noticed that no jam was available. She asked for jam, and the Mad Hatter said, "Jam is served every other day."

Alice protested, "But there was no jam yesterday either!"

"That's right," said the Mad Hatter. "The rule is: always jam yesterday and jam tomorrow, never jam today ... because today is not every other day!"

And that's how you are living: jam yesterday, jam tomorrow, never jam today. And that's where jam is! So you only imagine; you go on in a drugged, sleepy state. You have forgotten completely that this moment is the *only* real moment there is. And if you want to have any contact with reality, wake up herenow!

Hence this strange idea of Zen that enlightenment happens in an instant. Many people become puzzled: "How can it happen in an instant?" Indians particularly become very puzzled because they have the idea that first you have to get rid of all the past karmas, and now this foolish idea has reached to the West. Now in the West people are talking about past karma: first you have to get rid of the past karma.

Do you know how long the past is? It is eternity! And if you are to get rid of all past karma you are never going to get rid of it — that much is certain. And meanwhile you will be creating other karmas, and the past will go on becoming bigger and bigger every day. If that is the only way out — that one has to get rid of all past karmas — then there is no possibility of enlightenment. Then there has never been any Buddha and there is never going to be any Buddha; it is impossible. Just think of all the past lives and all the karmas that you have built up — first you have to get rid of them. And how are you going to get rid of them? In trying to get rid of them you will have to create other karmas. And this is a vicious circle.

"And to be totally enlightened," the people who believe in the philosophy of karma say, "not only are you to get rid of the bad karmas, you have to get rid of the good karmas too — because bad karmas create iron chains and good karmas create golden chains. But chains are chains, and you have to get rid of all kinds of chains." Now things become even more complicated. And how can you get rid of bad karmas? If you ask them they say, "Create good karma to get rid of bad karmas." And how can you get rid of good karmas? Then the saints become angry. They say, "Stop! You are arguing too much. This is not a question of argument. Believe, trust, have faith!"

It is not really a question of getting rid of karmas. When in the morning you wake up, do you have to get rid of all the dreams first? You have been a thief in the dreams, a murderer, a rapist, or a saint ... you can be all kinds of things in a dream. Do you have to get rid of all those dreams first? The *moment* you are awake you are out of all those dreams — they are finished! There is no question of getting rid of them.

That is the essential message of Zen: that you need not be worried about the past karmas; they were all dream acts. Just wake up and they are all finished.

But we are sleepy people and anything that fits with our sleep has great appeal. We listen only according to our state of mind. The whole world is asleep. There is rarely, once in a while, a person who is not asleep, who is awake. When he speaks to you there is misunderstanding, obviously. He speaks from his standpoint, from his awakening, and he says, "Forget all about your dreams — that is all nonsense! Good and bad, they are all alike; saint and sinner, they are all alike. Simply wake up! Don't be worried that first you have to become a saint in your dream, that you have to change your being a sinner into being a saint first, then you can wake up. Why go by such a long route? You can wake up directly! You can wake up while you are committing a sin; while you are murdering somebody in your dream you can wake up. There is no problem.

In fact, if you are a saint you may not like to wake up. A murderer will find it easier to wake up because he has

Take No Notice

nothing to lose, but the saint has great prestige to lose. Maybe he is being garlanded and a Nobel prize is being given and people are clapping and touching his feet ... and suddenly the alarm goes. Is this the time for the alarm? Can't the alarm wait a little more? When things are going so sweetly and beautifully the alarm can wait a little. A murderer has nothing to lose. He is already suffering; he is in a deep inner torture. In fact, he will feel relieved if the alarm goes off. He will feel a great freedom coming out of that nightmare.

Hence it happens more often that sinners wake up earlier than the saints, because the sinners go through nightmares and saints are having such sweet dreams. Who wants to wake up when you are a king with a golden palace and enjoying all kinds of things? Maybe you are in paradise in your dream.

But one thing is certain: when you are asleep you have a certain language — the language of sleep — and you can understand other people who are asleep and speak the same language. That's why the philosophy of karma became so important, so prevalent, so dominant. It has ruled almost all the religions of the world in different ways.

In India there have been three great religions: Hinduism, Jainism, Buddhism. They disagree on every point *except* on the philosophy of karma; they disagree on *every* point possible. They disagree on the existence of God, they disagree even on the existence of the soul, they disagree on the existence of the world, but they don't disagree on the philosophy of karma. It must have some deep appeal for the sleeping mind. And these people cannot understand Zen.

When a Hindu pundit or a Jaina *muni* comes to me he is very much puzzled. He says, "Are you teaching instant,

Try It My Way

sudden enlightenment? Then what about Mahavira who had to struggle for many many lives to become enlightened?"

I say to them, "Those stories are invented by you. The Mahavira that *you* talk about is an invention of your dream; you don't know about the real Mahavira. How can you know about his past lives? You don't even know about *your* past lives!" And there is not even any agreement on his last life amongst his followers — what to say about his past lives?

On such factual matters ... for example, whether he was married or not: one sect of Jainas says he was not married, because to them a man like Mahavira getting married looks insulting, humiliating. And the other sect of the Jainas says he was not only married, but he had a daughter too. Now that is going too far — having a daughter! That means he must have indulged in sex — because at that time the story of Jesus had not happened. Virgin birth was not yet known!

They can't agree ... the disciples can't agree about Mahavira's last life on factual matters like marriage, daughter, etcetera, and they talk about his past lives!

Anything that helps you to go on sleeping, postponing, appeals. "Even Mahavira had to work hard for many many lives, so how can *we* become enlightened in this life? It will take many lives, so there is no need to do anything right now. We can wait! And it is *not* going to happen right now anyway; it will take many many lives. Meanwhile, why not do other things? Accumulate more money, prestige, power. Do other things: eat, drink, be merry — because this is not going to happen, this enlightenment, right now; it will take many many lives. And meanwhile you cannot just go on sitting and waiting; one has to do something."

Sleeping people can understand a language which appeals to their sleep. We understand only that which triggers some process in our being.

The Sisters of Mercy were about to be sent as missionaries out into the world of sin. Mother Superior had one last question to ask each nun before deciding which of them were best fitted for the hazardous tasks ahead.

"Sister Agatha," she asked the first. "What would you do if you were walking along a deserted street at night and a strange man approached you and made indecent advances?"

"Oh, Holy Mother of God!" gasped the nun. "May all the saints forbid! Why, I would get down on my knees and pray to the Holy Virgin that my soul might be saved."

Mother Superior noted that Sister Agatha might be better suited to more domestic work.

The same question was asked of Sister Agnes, who replied, "Why, I would punch him in the nose ... and then start running down the street as fast as I could, shouting 'Help, help!'"

Mother Superior noted Sister Agnes as one of the possible candidates for the missionary work.

Next she asked Sister Theresa, who began, "Well, first I would pull his trousers down...." Mother Superior choked a little, but Sister Theresa continued. "And then I would pull my dress up, and then...."

"Sister Theresa," interrupted the senior nun. "Now what kind of an answer is that?"

"Well," said the other, "I just figure that I can run faster with my dress up than he can with his trousers down!"

We understand only that which we *can* understand. The sleeping humanity can understand only certain things; it can *hear* only certain things. The other things are not heard or even if heard they are not understood; they are misunderstood.

Try It My Way

Zen has been misunderstood very much. You will be surprised to know that even Buddhists don't understand Zen.

Many orthodox Buddhists have come to me asking why I emphasize Zen so much, because it is not the main Buddhist tradition. That is true; the main Buddhist tradition is against Zen. Zen seems to be a little outlandish, a little eccentric, for the simple reason that it brings such a totally new truth to you: *instant* enlightenment Never has any other religion emphasized it so much: that you are capable of becoming enlightened right now — it is all up to you.

If the training is efficient, enlightenment will be attained in one fingersnap.

There is no path as such, but there is a certain discipline to wake you up. That is called "training." Training has nothing to do with your character but something to do with your consciousness. Training simply means a certain space, a certain context has to be created around you in which awakening is easier than falling asleep — just like when you want somebody to be awake you throw cold water into his eyes. Not that you teach him to be virtuous, not that you teach him to be non-violent — those things are not going to help him to be awake. But cold water, that is a totally different phenomenon; that is creating a context. Or you give him a cup of tea; that helps him to wake up. Or you tell him to jog, run, shout; that will help him to wake up more quickly.

All Zen methods are like that: cold water thrown in your eyes, a hammer hit on your head. Zen is totally different from other religions. It does not give you a certain character; it certainly gives you a context.

Take No Notice

In days gone by, Ch'an Master Hui Chueh of Lang Yeh mountain, had a woman disciple who called on him for instruction. The Master taught her to examine into the sentence: "Take no notice."

NOW, THIS IS CREATING A CONTEXT. THE MASTER TOLD HER TO MEDITATE on this small sentence: "Take no notice." And it has to be meditated on in different situations, in all possible situations. It has not to be forgotten *any* time; it has to be remembered continuously, whatsoever happens.

She followed his instruction strictly without backsliding.

One day her house caught fire, but she said: "Take no notice."

Now, this is creating a context. This is real training, this is discipline. The house is on fire and she remembers the instruction: "Take no notice." It is easy when the house is not on fire and everything is running smoothly, well, and you can sit silently in a small corner you have made in the house to meditate — then you can say, "Take no notice." It is easy, but it is not going to wake you up; it may even help you to fall asleep. But when the house is on fire it is difficult, very difficult. Your possessiveness is at stake, your life is in danger, your security is gone, your safety is gone. You may be just a beggar the next day on the street with nothing left.

Try It My Way

But the woman must have been a real disciple.

She said: "Take no notice."

And not only did she say it, she *took* no notice. She relaxed, as if nothing was happening. And the moment you can see your house on fire and can see it as if nothing is happening, nothing happens. The house will be burned, but you will come out of that experience for the first time with clarity, with no dust on your mirror, with great insight. Everything is on fire! The whole life is on fire because we are dying every moment. Nothing is secure, nothing is safe. We only go on believing that everything is secure and safe. In this world of flux and change, where death is the ultimate end of everything, how can there be any security?

If you can see your own house on fire and go on meditating silently, relaxedly, in a deep let-go — *take no notice* — you will come out of it a totally different person, with a new consciousness, reborn.

Another day, her son fell into the water and when a bystander called her, she said, "Take no notice."

Now even more difficult — because a house is, after all, a dead thing. We can make another house, money can be earned again. But your son falls into the water, is drowning ... this is a more difficult situation, more attachment — your own son. And for the mother, the son is her extension, part of her, part of her soul, of her being. Still she says, "Take no notice."

She observed exactly her Master's instruction by laying down all casual thoughts.

If this is possible ... because these are the two problems in

Take No Notice

the world: possessiveness of things and relationship with people. These are *your* problems too. That's where people are asleep: either they are possessive with things or they are in heavy relationships with people. These are the two points which keep you clouded, confused, unaware.

She passed both the tests. And if you can pass these two things: if you can become aware that you possess nothing.... Use everything but possess nothing, and relate with people but don't become part of any relationship.

Relating is one thing, relationship quite another. Relating does not take you into any bondage; relationship is a bondage. Love people, but don't be jealous, don't be possessive. Relate with as many people as possible, but remain free and let them also be free of you. Don't try to dominate and don't allow anybody to dominate you either.

Use things, but remember: you come into the world with empty hands and you will go from the world again with empty hands, so you cannot possess anything.

If these two insights become clear and you start taking no note, all casual thoughts will disappear from your mind. And all thoughts are casual, no thought is essential. The essential is silence; thoughts are all casual. When thoughts disappear, the essential surfaces. Great silence explodes in a tremendous melody. And that experience is liberating, that experience is divine.

> *One day, as her husband lit the fire to make fritters of twisted dough, she threw into the pan full of boiling (vegetable) oil a batter which made a noise.*
>
> *Upon hearing the noise, she was instantly enlightened.*

Try It My Way

THAT'S WHAT I CALL ... IF YOU ARE READY, IF THE CONTEXT IS READY, then *anything* can trigger the process of enlightenment — *anything*. Just:

> *Upon hearing the noise, she was instantly enlightened.*

Nothing special was happening, just an ordinary noise. You come across that kind of noise every day many times. But if the right context is there, you are in a right space ... and she *was* in a right space: non-possessive, unrelated to anything, to any person, non-dominating. She was in a state of liberation, just on the borderline. One step more and she would move into the world of the Buddhas. And that small step can be caused by anything whatsoever.

> *Upon hearing the noise....*

That noise became the last alarm, the last straw on the back of the camel.

> *...she was instantly enlightened. Then she threw the pan of oil on the ground, clapped her hands and laughed.*

Why did she do that: *clapped her hands and laughed?* When one becomes enlightened, laughter is almost a natural by-product; spontaneously it comes — for the simple reason that we have been searching and searching for lives for something which was already there inside. Our whole effort was ridiculous! Our whole effort was absurd. One laughs at the great cosmic joke. One laughs at the sense of humor that God must have or the existence: that we have

Take No Notice

it with us already and we are searching for it. One laughs at one's own ridiculous efforts, long long journeys, pilgrimages, for something which was never lost in the first place. Hence the laughter, hence the clapping.

> *Thinking she was insane, her husband scolded her and said...*

And of course, anybody who is still asleep seeing somebody suddenly becoming enlightened, clapping hands and laughing, is bound to think that the person has gone insane. This *breakthrough* will look to the sleeping person like a break*down*; it is not a break-down. But the sleeping person can't help it; he can understand only according to his values, criterions.

> *...he scolded her and said: "Why do you do this? Are you mad?"*
>
> *She replied: "Take no notice."*

She continues: her meditation is still there. She is following her Master's instruction to the very end. The husband is calling her mad and she says: "Take no notice."

The world *will* call you mad. The world has always been calling Buddhas mad. Take no notice. It is natural; it should be accepted as a matter of course.

> *Then she went to Master Hui Chueh and asked him to verify her achievement.*

THE MASTER'S FUNCTIONS ARE MANY. FIRST: TO HELP YOU TO WAKE UP, to provoke you into an awakening; to create the situation in which sleep becomes more and more difficult and awakening becomes more and more easy; and when for the first time you *are* awakened, to confirm it, because it is very difficult for the person himself. The territory is so unknown. The ego is lost, all old values are gone, the old mind is no more functioning. Everything is so new; nothing seems to be continuous with the old. There seems to be no way to judge, evaluate, be certain. One *is* in deep awe and wonder. One does not know what is happening, what has happened, what it is all about. One is simply at a loss.

Hence the last function of the Master is to confirm, to say, "Yes, this is it."

The Master confirmed that she had obtained the holy fruit.

Zen people call this "the holy fruit," the fruition, the flowering — coming to the ultimate awakening, coming to the ultimate experience of yourself and existence. But remember: it can only happen in the moment. It can only happen in the instant. It can only happen now — now or never.

You will ask: "Then why all these methods, trainings?" They are just to bring you back to the now. You have gone too far away in the memories and in imagination. They are not to create any cultivation; they are not for self-cultivation but for bringing you back home.

Here we are using all kinds of methods, and as many more people will be coming we will be devising new methods, because different people will need different methods. In the new commune we are going to have all possible methods. It has never been tried on such a scale. Every religion has a few methods, but we are going to have *all* the methods of all the religions of the past and of all the religions that are going to happen in the future. We are going to create a space for *all* kinds of people, not for any particular type. The old religions are missing in that way.

For example, only a particular type of person can be helped by Mahavira's methods — only the type who belongs to Mahavira's type can be helped. It is a very limited methodology. Mahavira attained to the holy fruit; he taught the same method by which he attained. Jesus had his own method, Mohammed had his own method. So no religion of the past could be universal because it belonged to a certain type and only that type could be benefited by it.

Hence one problem has arisen: you may be born in a Jaina family and you may not be of the same type which the Jaina method can help. Then you are in a difficulty; your whole life will be a wastage. You will try the method; it won't suit you — and you will not change your method. You will think it is because of your past karmas that the method is not working, that it will take time. You will rationalize. You may be born in a Hindu family and Hindu methods may not work.

There are so many types of people in the world, and as the world has grown and people's consciousnesses have grown, more and more new types, more and more crossbreeds have come into existence which were never there before — which never existed in Mahavira's time, which never existed in Krishna's time. There are many new types, crossbreeds. And in the future this is going to happen more and more; the world is becoming a small village.

My effort is to use all the methods of the past, to make them up-to-date, to make them contemporary, and to create new methods for the future — for the future of humanity. Hence what I am teaching is neither Hinduism nor Buddhism nor Christianity, and yet I am teaching the essence of all the religions.

You are here not to cultivate a certain spiritual ego but to dissolve all the ego, to dissolve all sleep. You are here to wake up. The situation is being created — use this situation as totally as possible.

Remember this woman who was meditating on "Take no notice." Such totality is needed. The house is on fire and she says: "Take no notice." Her son falls into the water and she says: "Take no notice." Her husband calls her mad and she says: "Take no notice." Then such a simple meditation — of taking no notice — creates the necessary milieu in which she becomes aflame, afire. Her inner being explodes. She is no more the same old person; she is reborn. She is reborn as enlightened. She becomes a Buddha.

You are all Buddhas — sleeping, dreaming, but you are Buddhas all the same. My function is not to *make* Buddhas out of you, because you are already that, but just to help you remember it, to remind you.

Not Knowing Is The Most Intimate

The first question
Osho,

Is awareness a higher value than love?

Virendra,

THE HIGHEST PEAK IS THE CULMINATION OF ALL THE VALUES: TRUTH, love, awareness, authenticity, totality. At the highest peak they are indivisible. They are separate only in the dark valleys of our unconsciousness. They are separate only when they are polluted, mixed with other things. The moment they become pure they become one; the more pure, the closer they come to each other.

For example, each value exists on many planes; each value is a ladder of many rungs. Love is lust — the lowest rung, which touches hell; and love is also prayer — the highest rung, which touches paradise. And between these two there are many planes easily discernible.

In lust, love is only one percent; ninety-nine percent are other things: jealousies, ego trips, possessiveness, anger, sexuality. It is more physical, more chemical; it has nothing deeper than that. It is very superficial, not even skin-deep.

Try It My Way

As you go higher, things become deeper; they start having new dimensions. That which was only physiological starts having a psychological dimension to it. That which was nothing but biology starts becoming psychology. We share biology with all the animals; we don't share psychology with all the animals.

When love goes still higher — or deeper, which is the same — then it starts having something of the spiritual in it. It becomes metaphysical. Only Buddhas, Krishnas, Christs, they know that quality of love.

Love is spread all the way and so are other values. When love is one hundred percent pure you cannot make any distinction between love and awareness; then they are no more two. You cannot make any distinction between love and God even; they are no more two. Hence Jesus' statement that God is love. He makes them synonymous. There is great insight in it.

On the periphery everything appears separate from everything else; on the periphery existence is many. As you come closer to the center, the manyness starts melting, dissolving, and oneness starts arising. At the center, everything is one.

Hence your question, Virendra, is right only if you don't understand the highest quality of love and awareness. It is absolutely irrelevant if you have any glimpse of the Everest, of the highest peak.

You ask: *Is awareness a higher value than love?*
There is nothing higher and nothing lower. In fact, there are not two values at all. These are the two paths from the valley leading to the peak. One path is of awareness, meditation: the path of Zen we have been talking about these days. And the other is the path of love, the path of the devotees, the *bhaktas,* the Sufis. These two paths are sepa-

Not Knowing Is The Most Intimate

rate when you start the journey; you have to choose. Whichever you choose is going to lead to the same peak. And as you come closer to the peak you will be surprised: the travelers on the other path are coming closer to you. Slowly slowly, the paths start merging into each other. By the time you have reached the ultimate, they are one.

The person who follows the path of awareness finds love as a consequence of his awareness, as a by-product, as a shadow. And the person who follows the path of love finds awareness as a consequence, as a by-product, as a shadow of love. They are two sides of the same coin.

And remember: if your awareness lacks love then it is still impure; it has not yet known one hundred percent purity. It is not yet *really* awareness; it must be mixed with unawareness. It is not pure light; there must be pockets of darkness inside you still working, functioning, influencing you, dominating you. If your love is without awareness, then it is not love yet. It must be something lower, something closer to lust than to prayer.

So let it be a criterion: if you follow the path of awareness, let love be the criterion. When your awareness suddenly blooms into love, know perfectly well that awareness has happened, *samadhi* has been achieved. If you follow the path of love, then let awareness function as a criterion, as a touchstone. When suddenly, from nowhere, at the very center of your love. a flame of awareness starts arising, know perfectly well ... rejoice! You have come home.

Try It My Way

The second question

Why, Osho, isn't knowledge of the scriptures helpful in finding the truth?

Maneeshi,

KNOWLEDGE IS NOT YOURS, THAT'S WHY. IT IS BORROWED. AND CAN YOU borrow truth? Truth is untransferable; nobody can give it to you. Not even an alive Master can transmit it to you. You can learn, but it cannot be taught. So what to say about dead scriptures, howsoever holy they may be? They must have come from some original source; some Master, someone awakened must have been at the very source of them — but now they are only words. They are only words about truth, information about truth.

To be with Krishna is a totally different matter from reading the Bhagavad Gita. To be with Mohammed, attuned, in deep harmony, overlapping with his being, allowing his being to stir and move your heart, is one thing. And just to read the Koran is a far, faraway cry; it is an echo in the mountains. It is not the truth itself; it is a reflection, a full moon reflected in the lake. If you jump into the lake you are not going to get to the moon; in fact, if you jump into the lake even the reflection will disappear. Scriptures are only mirrors reflecting faraway truths.

Now the Vedas have existed for at least five thousand years; they reflect something five thousand years old. Much dust has gathered on the mirror, much interpretation, commentary — that's what I mean by dust. Now you cannot know exactly what the Vedas say; you know only the commentators, the interpreters, and they are thousands. There

Not Knowing Is The Most Intimate

is a thick wall of commentaries and it is impossible to just put it aside. You will know only *about* truth, and not only that: you will know commentaries and interpretations of people who have not experienced at all.

Knowledge is imparted for other purposes. Yes, there is a possibility of imparting knowledge about the world because the world is outside you, it is objective. Science is knowledge; science, the very word, means exactly knowledge. But religion is not knowledge.

Religion is experience — for the simple reason that its whole concern is your interiority, your subjectivity, which is available only to you and to nobody else. You cannot invite even your beloved into your inner being. There you are utterly alone — and there resides the truth.

Knowledge will go on enhancing, decorating, enriching your memory, but not your being. Your being is a totally different phenomenon. In fact, knowledge will create barriers. One has to unlearn all that one has learned — only then does one reach the being. One has to be innocent. *Not knowing is the most intimate.* Knowing creates distance.

You ask me, Maneeshi: *Why isn't knowledge of the scriptures helpful in finding the truth?*

For the simple reason that if you accumulate knowledge you will be starting to believe in conclusions. You will already conclude what truth is without *knowing* it, and your conclusion will become the greatest hindrance. Truth has to be approached in utter nudity, in utter purity, in silence, in a state of innocence, child-like wonder and awe; not knowing already, not full of the rubbish called knowledge, not full of the Vedas and the Bibles and the Korans, but utterly silent ... without any thought, without any conclusion, without knowing anything about truth. When you approach in this way, suddenly truth is revealed. And truth is revealed here and now: *"Ah, this!"* A great rejoicing starts happening inside you.

Truth is not separate from you; it is your innermost core. So you need not to learn it from somebody else. Then what's the function of the Masters?

The function of the Masters is to help you drop your knowledge, to help you unlearn, to help you towards a state of unconditioning. Your knowledge means you will be always looking through a curtain and that curtain will distort everything. And knowledge is dead. Consciousness is needed, knowing is needed, a state of seeing is needed, but not knowledge. How can you know the alive through the dead?

A man stepped into a very crowded bus. After a while he took out his glass eye, threw it up in the air, then put it back in again. Ten minutes later he again took out his glass eye, threw it up in the air, then put it back in again.

The lady next to him was horrified. "What are you doing?" she cried.

"I am just trying to see if there is any room up front."

That's what knowledge is: a glass eye. You cannot see through it, it is impossible to see through it.

Drop all your conclusions — Hindu, Christian, Mohammedan, Jaina, Jewish. Drop all the knowledge that has been forced upon you. Every child has been poisoned — poisoned by knowledge, poisoned by the parents, the society, the church, the state. Every child has been distracted from his innocence, from his not-knowing. And that's why every child, slowly slowly, becomes so burdened that he loses all joy of life, all ecstasy of being, and he becomes just like the crowd, part of the crowd.

In fact, the moment a child is perfectly conditioned by you, you are very happy; you call it "religious education."

Not Knowing Is The Most Intimate

You are very happy that the child has been initiated into the religion of his parents. All that you have done is you have destroyed his capacity to know on his own. You have destroyed his authenticity. You have destroyed his very precious innocence. You have closed his doors and windows. Now he will live an encapsulated existence. He will live in his inner darkness, surrounded by all kinds of stupid theories, systems of thought, philosophies, ideologies. He will be lost in a jungle of words and he will not be able to come out of it easily.

Even if he comes across a Master, if he meets a Buddha, then too it will take years for him to unlearn — because learning becomes almost your blood, your bones, your marrow. And to go against your own knowledge seems to be going against yourself, against your tradition, against your country, against your religion. It seems as if you are a traitor, as if you are betraying. In fact, your society has betrayed you, has contaminated your soul.

Every society has been doing that up to now, and every society has been very successfully doing it. That's why it is so rare to find a Buddha; it is so rare to escape from the traps the society puts all around the child. And the child is so unaware; he can easily be conditioned, hypnotized. And that's what goes on and on in the temples, in the churches, in the schools, colleges, universities. They all serve the past; they don't serve the future. Their function is to perpetuate the past, the dead past.

My work here is just the opposite. I am not here to perpetuate the past; hence I am against all knowledge. I am all for learning, but learning means innocence, learning means openness, learning means receptivity. Learning means a non-egoistic approach towards reality. Learning means: "I don't know and I am ready — ready to know."

Try It My Way

Knowledge means: "I know already." Knowledge is the greatest deception that society creates in people's minds.

My function is to serve the future, not the past. The past is no more, but the future is coming every moment. I want you to become innocent, seers, knowers — not knowledgeable — alert, aware, not unconsciously clinging to conclusions.

The third question
Osho,

Why does it take so long for me to get it?
Pankaja,

IT IS BECAUSE OF YOUR KNOWLEDGE. PANKAJA HAS WRITTEN MANY BOOKS; she has been a well-known author. And here I have given her the work of cleaning. In the beginning it was very hurtful to her ego. She must have been hoping some day to get a Nobel prize! And she has been wondering what she is doing here. Her books have been praised and appreciated, and rather than giving her some work nourishing to her ego I have given her very ego-shattering work: cleaning the toilets of the ashram. It was difficult for her to swallow, but she is a courageous soul, she swallowed it. And slowly slowly she has become relaxed.

Pankaja, it is not special to you; it takes time for everybody. And the more successful you have been in life, the more it takes for you to get it, because your very success is nothing but a prop, a new prop for the ego — and ego is the barrier. The ego has to be shattered, uprooted totally, smashed, burned, so nothing remains of it. It is arduous work, hard work.

And sometimes it looks as if the Master is cruel. But the Master has to be cruel because he loves you, because he has compassion for you. It may appear paradoxical in the beginning — because if you have compassion, then you can't be cruel. That is the complexity of the work: that if the Master is really compassionate he cannot sympathize with anything that nourishes your ego.

So I have been in every way shattering Pankaja's ego. She has been crying and weeping and freaking out ... but slowly slowly things have settled. The storm is no more and a great silence has come in.

In fact, if you think of your many past lives — such a long long sleep, such a long long dreaming — then just being here with me for two, three years is not a long time if the silence has started permeating your being. Even if it happens in thirty years' time it is happening soon.

Many people come to me and ask, "Osho, when is *my* satori going to happen?"

I say, "very soon" — but remember what I mean by "very soon." It may take thirty years, forty years, fifty years, but that is very soon. Looking at your long long journey of darkness, if within thirty years we can create the light it is really as fast as it can be.

But things are happening far more quickly. Every situation is being created here so processes can be quickened. It is not too late, Pankaja, it is too early. And I can see the change happening. The spring is not far away; the first flowers have already appeared.

In fact, this was your vocation, but it took so many years of your life to reach me. What you were doing before you came to me was not really part of your heart; it was just a head trip — hence it was not a fulfillment. Successful you could become; famous, yes, that was possible. But it would not have been a contentment, it would not have been a deep deep joy — because unless something that belongs to your heart starts growing, contentment is not possible, fulfillment is not possible.

Now you are on the right track. Now things will happen with a faster pace. Speed also is accumulative. If you have watched the spring, first only one flower blooms, and then ten flowers, then hundreds of flowers, and then thousands, and then millions...

Just like that it happens in spiritual growth too. But everybody is stumbling in darkness, groping in darkness. Somebody becomes a poet not knowing whether that is his vocation, his heart's real desire. Somebody becomes a musician not knowing whether that is going to fulfill his life. Somebody becomes a painter.... And people have to become something; some earning is needed and one has to do something to prove oneself. So people go on groping and they become something.

And you are fortunate, Pankaja, that you came to realize that what you were doing was not the real thing for you. There are many unfortunate people — after their whole lives are wasted, then they recognize that they have been into something which was not their real work. They were doing somebody else's work.

I have heard about a famous surgeon, one of the world's most famous surgeons. He was retiring. Even at the age of seventy-five his hands were as young as they had been before. He was able to do brain surgery even at the age of seventy-five; his hands were not yet shaky.

Everybody was happy — his disciples, students, colleagues — and they were celebrating. But he was sad.

Not Knowing Is The Most Intimate

Somebody asked him, "Why are you sad? You are the world's most famous brain surgeon. You should be happy!"

He said, "Yes, I should be happy, I also think so, but what can I do? I never wanted to be a famous surgeon in the first place. I wanted to be a dancer — and I am the lousiest dancer you can find. My father *forced* me to be a surgeon — and he was right in a way, because by dancing what can you get? The very idea was silly in his eyes, so he forced me to be a surgeon. I became a surgeon, I became famous. Now I am retiring, but I am sad — my whole life has gone down the drain. I never wanted to be a surgeon in the first place, so who cares whether I am famous or not? I would have loved to be just a good dancer, even if unknown, anonymous — that would have been enough."

While questioning a suspect, the police detective leafed through the man's folder. "I see here," he said, "that you have a string of previous arrests. Here is one for armed robbery, breaking and entering, sexual assault, sexual assault, sexual assault...."

"Yes, sir," replied the fellow modestly, "it took me a little while to find out what I do best."

Pankaja, you came to me in the right time. Rejoice! Celebrate! And things have started happening. You were like a hard rock when you came; now you are becoming soft like a flower. The spring is not far away.

Try It My Way

The fourth question

Osho,

Most religions have a negative attitude towards work, as if it is a punishment and a labor and not at all spiritual. Could you speak to us more about working?

Parmananda,

THE BUDDHAS HAVE ALWAYS BEEN LIFE-AFFIRMATIVE, BUT THE RELIGIONS that arose afterwards have all been life-negative. This is a strange phenomenon, but there is something which has to be understood — why it happened in the first place. And it happened again and again.

It seems that the moment a Buddha speaks he is bound to be misunderstood. If you don't understand him, that's okay, but people don't stop there: they *mis*understand him — because people cannot tolerate the idea that they don't understand. It is better to misunderstand than not to understand; at least you have some kind of understanding. All the Buddhas have been misunderstood, wrongly interpreted. And whatsoever they were standing for has been forgotten as soon as they were gone, and just the opposite was organized.

Jesus was a lover of life, a very affirmative person, but Christianity is life-negative. The seers of the Upanishads were absolutely life-affirmative people, they loved life tremendously, but Hinduism is life-negative, Buddhism and Jainism are life-negative.

Just look at the statue of Mahavira and you will see that he must have loved his body, he must have loved life and existence. He is so beautiful! It is said about Mahavira that it is possible that never before and never again has a more beautiful person walked on the earth. But look at the Jaina *munis*, the Jaina monks, and you will find them the ugliest. What has happened?

Buddha is very life-affirmative. Of course, he does not affirm *your* life, because your life is not life at all; it is death in disguise. He *condemns* your life, but he affirms the real life, the eternal life. But that's how he was misunderstood. His condemnation of your false life was taken to be condemnation of life itself. And nobody bothered that he was affirming life — real life, eternal life, divine life, the life of the awakened ones. That is true life. What life do *you* have? It is just a nightmarish experience. But the Buddhists — the Buddhist monks and nuns — have lived *against* life.

Parmananda, it is because of this misunderstanding, which seems to be inevitable.... I can see it happening with me. Whatsoever I say is immediately misunderstood all over the world. I really enjoy it! Strange, but somehow seems to be natural. The moment you say something you can be sure that it is going to be misunderstood, for the simple reason that people are going to interpret it according to *their* minds. And their minds are fast asleep. They are hearing in their sleep; they can't hear rightly, they can't hear the whole thing. Only fragments they hear.

Even a man like P.D. Ouspensky, who lived with Gurdjieff for years, could not hear the whole teaching as it was. When he wrote his famous book *In Search of the Miraculous* and he showed it to George Gurdjieff, his Master, he said, "It is beautiful, but it needs a subtitle: *Fragments of an Unknown Teaching.*"

Try It My Way

Ouspensky said, "But why? — why fragments?"

He said, "Because these are only fragments. What I have told you you have not heard in its totality. And whatsoever you have written is beautiful...."

Ouspensky was really one of the most skillful writers the world has ever known, very artistic, very logical, a superb artist with words.

So he said, "You have written well, you have written beautifully, but these are only fragments — and the fragments cannot reveal the truth. On the contrary, they conceal it. So call it: *Fragments of an Unknown Teaching*. The teaching still remains unknown. You just had a few glimpses here and there, and you have put all those glimpses together, you have somehow made a whole out of them, but it is not the truth, it is not the real teaching."

Ouspensky understood it. Hence the book still carries the subtitle: *Fragments of an Unknown Teaching*.

What to say about ordinary people? Ouspensky cannot be called an ordinary person; extraordinarily intelligent he was. In fact, it was because of him that Gurdjieff became famous in the world; otherwise nobody may have heard about him. His own writings are very difficult to understand. There are very few people in the world who have read *his* books — they are very difficult to read. Gurdjieff writes in such a way that he makes it in every possible way difficult for you to grasp what he is saying, what he wants to say. Sentences go on and on ... by the time the sentence comes to a full stop you have forgotten the beginning! And he uses words of his own invention which exist nowhere; nobody knows what the meaning of those words is. No dictionary has those words. In fact, they never existed before; he invented them.

And he writes in such a boring way that if you suffer

Not Knowing Is The Most Intimate

from insomnia they are good, those books. You read three ... four pages at the most you can read and you are bound to fall asleep. I have never come across a single person who has read his books from the beginning to the end.

When for the first time his first book was published — *All and Everything* — one hundred pages were open and the remaining nine hundred pages were not cut yet. And with a note the book was sold saying, "Read the first hundred pages, the introductory part. If you still feel like reading, then you can open the other pages. Otherwise return the book and take your money back." Even to read those hundred pages is very difficult.

It was a device. It needs great awareness to read. The book is not written to inform you about something; the book is only a device to make you aware. You can read it only if you are very conscious, if you have decided consciously, "I have to go through it from the beginning to the end, and I am not going to fall asleep, and I am not going to stop, whatsoever happens, and whatsoever my mind says I am going to finish it."

If you make that decision ... and it is very difficult to keep it for one thousand pages of such nonsense. Yes, here and there there are beautiful truths, but then you will come across those truths only if you go through much nonsense. Gems you will find, but they are few and far between. Once in a while you will come across a diamond, but for that you will have to read fifty, sixty very boring pages.

I have seen thousands of books, but Gurdjieff is extraordinary. Nobody have I seen who can create such boring stuff. But he is deliberately doing it; that was his method.

If you went to see him, the first thing he would tell you was to read fifty pages of his book loudly in front of him.

Try It My Way

That was the greatest task! You don't understand a single word, a single sentence, and it goes on and on and on, and he sits there looking at you. You have to finish fifty pages, then you can be accepted as a disciple. If you cannot manage this simple feat, then you are rejected.

Ouspensky made him famous in the world, but even Ouspensky could not get to the very core of his teaching — only fragments. And he understood only in part.

And remember always: truth cannot be divided into fragments; you cannot understand only parts of it. Either you understand the whole of it or you don't understand it at all. But it is very difficult to recognize the fact that "I don't understand." And knowledgeable people — scholars, professors — they can*not* accept that *they* don't understand, so they go on misinterpreting.

And the most fatal misinterpretation has been that all affirmative teachings have been turned into negative ones. In fact, you live in a negative darkness. When Buddha speaks he speaks from a positive state of light; by the time his words reach you they have reached into a negative darkness. Your negative darkness changes the color of those words, the meaning of those words, the connotations of those words, the nuances of those words. And then *you* create the church. You create Christianity, Hinduism, Mohammedanism, Jainism; you create all kinds of "isms" and you create all kinds of religions.

Yes, Parmananda, most religions have a negative attitude towards work because they are against life. Hence they can't be *for* work, they can't be creative. They teach renunciation of life — how can they teach creativity? And they teach that life is a punishment, so how can they say life is spiritual? You are being punished for your past life karmas, that's why you are born. It is a punishment — just as in

Not Knowing Is The Most Intimate

Soviet Russia if you are punished you are sent to Siberia.

In the days of the British Raj in India, if somebody was to be really punished they used to send him to faraway islands: Andaman, Nicobar. The climate is bad, not healthy at all; no facilities to live, nothing grows, hard work. That was punishment.

All these life-negative religions have been telling you, directly or indirectly, that this earth is like Andaman and Nicobar, or like Siberia, and you are prisoners. You have been thrown here, thrown into life, to be punished. This is utter nonsense.

Life is not a prison, it is a school. You are sent here to learn, you are sent here to grow. You are sent here to become more conscious, more aware. This earth is a great device of God.

This is *my* approach towards life: life is not a punishment but a reward. You are rewarded by being given a great opportunity to grow, to see, to know, to understand, to be. I call life spiritual. In fact, to me, life and God are synonymous.

The fifth question
Osho,

Why do Indians think they are more spiritual than others?

John,

PLEASE FORGIVE THE POOR INDIANS. THEY DON'T HAVE ANYTHING ELSE to brag about. You can brag about other things: money,

Try It My Way

power, atomic or hydrogen bombs, airplanes, that you have walked on the moon, that you have penetrated to the very secrets of life, your science, technology; you can brag about your affluence. Poor India has nothing else to brag about; it can only brag about something invisible so there is no need to prove it. Spirituality is such a thing you can brag about it and nobody can prove it, nobody can disprove it.

For thousands of years India has suffered starvation, poverty, so much so that it has to rationalize it. It has rationalized it so that to be poor is something spiritual. The Indian spiritual man renounces all comforts and becomes poor. When he becomes poor, only then do Indians recognize him as spiritual. If he does not become poor, how can he be spiritual?

Poverty has become the very foundation of Indian spirituality. The more poor you are, the more spiritual you are. Even if you are unhealthy, that is good for being spiritual; that shows your antagonism towards the body. Torture your body, fast, don't eat, don't fulfill the needs of the body, and you are doing some spiritual work.

So you will look at Indian so-called spiritual saints and many of them will look physically ill, in deep suffering, in self-torture; their faces are pale because of fasting. But if you ask their disciples they will say, "Look, what a golden aura around the face of our saint!" I know such people — just a feverish aura around their faces, nothing else! But their disciples will say, "A golden aura — this is spirituality!"

Count Keyserling writes in his diary that when he came to India he understood for the first time that poverty, starvation, ill health, these are necessary requirements for spirituality. These are rationalizations. And everybody wants to be higher than the other, superior to the other.

Not Knowing Is The Most Intimate

Now, there is no other way for Indians to declare their superiority. They cannot compete in science, in technology, in industry, but they can compete in spirituality. They are more able to fast, to starve themselves. For thousands of years they have practiced starvation, so they have become very very accustomed to it; it is easy for them.

For the American to go on a fast is very difficult. Eating five times a day — that means almost the whole day you are eating — and I am not counting things that you eat in between.... For the American it is difficult to fast, but for the Indian it has become almost natural. His body has become accustomed to it. The body has a tremendous capacity to adjust itself.

The Indian can sit in the hot sun, almost in a state of fire from the showering of the sun, undisturbed. You cannot sit there — you have become accustomed to air-conditioning. The Indian can sit in the cold weather, naked in the Himalayas. *You* cannot; you have become accustomed to central heating. The body becomes accustomed.

And then India can claim: "This is spirituality. Come and compete with us!" And you cannot compete. And certainly, when you cannot compete, you have to bow down to the Indians and you have to accept that they must have some clue. There is no clue, nothing, just a long long history of poverty.

In a cannibal village in the heart of Africa, the wife of the chief head-hunter went to the local butcher's shop in search of a choice rib for her husband's dinner. Inspecting the goods, she asked the butcher, "What is that one?"

The butcher replied, "That is an American — seventy cents a pound."

"Well, then what about that one?" asked the woman.

The butcher replied, "That is an Italian — ninety-five cents a pound. He is a little spicy."

Try It My Way

"And," asked the woman, "what about that one there in the corner?"

"He is an Indian," replied the butcher. "two dollars a pound."

The woman gasped, "Two dollars a pound? What makes him so expensive?"

"Well, lady," the butcher replied, "have you ever tried cleaning an Indian?"

But that has become spirituality. Do you know? — Jaina monks never take a bath. To take a bath is thought to be a luxury. They don't clean their teeth; that is thought to be a luxury. Now, to be spiritual in the Jaina sense of the term you have to stop taking a bath, cleaning your teeth, even combing your hair, even cutting your hair. If it becomes too messy, too dirty, you have to pull it out by hand. You can't use any razor or any other mechanical device, because a spiritual person should be independent of all machines. So Jaina monks pull their own hair out. And when a Jaina monk pulls his hair out, mostly once a year, then a great gathering happens because it is thought to be something very special.

I have been to such gatherings. Thousands of Jainas gather together simply to see this poor man, hungry, dirty, pulling his hair out — crazy! And you will see people watching with great joy and with great superiority: "This is our saint! Who *else* can compete with us?"

No nation is spiritual. It has not happened yet. One can hope that it may happen some day, but it has not happened yet. In fact, only individuals can be spiritual, not nations. And individuals have been spiritual all over the world, everywhere. But ignorance prevents people from recognizing others' spirituality.

One day I was talking to an Indian and I told him that

Not Knowing Is The Most Intimate

everywhere spirituality has been happening; it is nothing to do with India as such.

He said, "But so many saints have happened here. Where else have so many saints happened?"

I said, "Do you know how many saints have happened in China? Just tell me a few names."

He had not even heard of a single name. He does not know anything about Lao Tzu, he does not know about Chuang Tzu, he does not know about Lieh Tzu. He does not know anything of the long long tradition of Chinese mysticism. But he knows about Nanak, Kabir, Mahavira, Krishna, Buddha, so he thinks all the great saints have happened only in India. That is sheer stupidity. They have happened in Japan, they have happened in Egypt, they have happened in Jerusalem. They have happened everywhere! But you don't know — and you don't want to know either. You simply remain confined to your own sect.

In fact, you may have lived in the neighborhood of the Jainas your whole life, but you cannot tell the twenty-four names of their great *teerthankaras*. Who bothers to know about the others? Only one name — Mahavira — is known; the twenty-three other names are almost unknown. Even Jainas themselves cannot give the twenty-four names in exact sequence. They know three names: the first, Adinatha; the last, Mahavira; and the one before Mahavira, a cousin-brother of Krishna, Neminath. These three are known; the remaining twenty-one are almost unknown even to the Jainas. And this is how it is.

Do you know how many Hassid mystics have attained to God? Do you know how many Zen Masters have attained to Buddhahood? Do you know how many Sufis have attained to the ultimate state? Nobody cares, nobody wants to know. People live in a small, cozy corner of their own religion and they think this is all.

Neither Indians nor anybody else is specially spiritual or holy. Spirituality is something that happens to individuals. It is the individual becoming aflame with God. It has nothing to do with any collectivity — nation, race, church.

The sixth question
Osho,

Why are the Jews so notorious for their money-greed?

Narotam,

DO YOU THINK OTHERS ARE IN ANY WAY DIFFERENT FROM THE JEWS? Unless love flowers in your being you are bound to remain greedy. Greed is the absence of love. If you love, greed disappears; if you don't love, greed remains.

Greed is rooted in fear. And of course, Jews have lived in tremendous fear for centuries. For the two thousand years since Jesus they have lived in constant fear. Fear creates greed. And because they lost their nation — they lost everything, they became uprooted, they became wanderers — the only thing they could trust was money; they could not trust anybody else. Hence, naturally, they became greedy. Don't be too hard on them for that. They are greedy, maybe a little more than others, but that is only a difference of quantity, not of quality.

In India we have *Marwaris,* who are the Indian Jews. Jainas are not less greedy ... and others too! Maybe they are not so notorious. Jews become notorious because whatsoever they do, they do with a flavor; whatsoever they do, they do without any disguise. They are not very deceptive people — intelligent but not deceptive. Whatsoever they want to do, they do it directly. And they are very earthly people. And that is one of the qualities I appreciate. The earth is our home and we have to be earthly.

A real spirituality must be rooted in earthliness. Any spirituality that denies the earth, rejects the earth, becomes abstract, becomes airy-fairy. It has no more blood in it; it is no more alive. Yes, Jews are very earth-bound.

And what is wrong in having money? One should not be possessive; one should be able to use it. And Jews know how to use it! One should not be miserly. Money has to be created and money has to be used. Money is a beautiful invention, a great blessing, if rightly used. It makes many things possible. Money is a magical phenomenon.

If you have a ten-rupee note in your pocket, you have thousands of things in your pocket. You can have anything with those ten rupees. You can materialize a man who will massage your body the whole night! Or you can materialize food or you can materialize *anything!* That ten-rupee note carries many possibilities. You cannot carry all those possibilities with you if there is no note; then your life will be very limited. You can have a man who can massage your body, but then that is the only possibility you have with you. If you suddenly feel hungry or thirsty, then that man cannot do anything else. But a ten-rupee note can do many things, millions of things; it has infinite possibilities. It is one of the greatest inventions of man; there is no need to be against it. *I* am not against it.

Use it. Don't cling to it. Clinging is bad. The more you cling to money, the poorer the world becomes because of your clinging, because money is multiplied if it is always moving from one hand to another hand.

Try It My Way

In English we have another name for money which is more significant — it is "currency". That simply indicates that money should always remain moving like a current. It should always be on the move from one hand to another hand. The more it moves the better.

For example, if I have a ten-rupee note and I keep it to myself, then there is only one ten-rupee note in the world. If I give it to you and you give it to somebody else and each person goes on giving, if it goes through ten hands then we have a hundred rupees, we have used a hundred rupees' worth of utilities; the ten rupees is multiplied by ten.

And Jews know how to use money; nothing is wrong in it. Yes, greed is bad. Greed means you become obsessed with money; you don't use it as a means, it becomes the end. That is bad, and it is bad whether you are a Jew or a Jaina, Hindu or Mohammedan; it doesn't matter.

Four Jewish mothers were talking, naturally of their sons.

One said, "My son is studying to be a doctor, and when he graduates he will make $50,000 a year."

Said the second, "My son is studying dentistry, and when he graduates he will make $100,000 a year."

The third said, "My son is studying to be a psychoanalyst, and when he graduates he will make $200,000 a year."

The fourth one remained silent. The other ones asked her, "And what about your son?"

"He is studying to become a rabbi," she answered.

"And how much does a rabbi make?"

"$10,000 a year."

"$10,000? Is this a job for a jewish boy?"

Gropestein's clothing store stood on New York's Lower East Side. One day, Gropestein went out for lunch and left

Not Knowing Is The Most Intimate

Salter, his new salesman, in charge. When he came back Salter proudly announced, "I sold that black cloth coat."

"For how much?" asked Gropestein.

"Ninety-eight cents, like it said on the tag."

"Ninety-eight cents?" screamed the owner. "The tag said ninety-eight dollars, you idiot!"

The clerk looked as if he would die of embarrassment.

"Let this be a lesson to you," said Gropestein. "But don't feel bad — we made ten percent profit."

A famous anti-Semite was dying. He gathered his sons around his deathbed and said, "Sons, my last wish and command is that whenever you need anything, go buy it from a Jew and give him the first price he asks."

The sons in surprise said, "Father, has your mind gone crazy in this your last hour?"

"Ah, no," smiled the anti-Semite wickedly, "he is going to eat himself up he has not asked for more."

The seventh question
Osho,

What is the future of morality concerning sex?

Divendra,

THERE IS NO FUTURE OF ANY MORALITY CONCERNING SEX. IN FACT, THE very combination of sex and morality has poisoned the whole past of morality. Morality became so much sex-oriented that it lost all other dimensions — which are far more important. Sex should not really be so much of a concern for moral thinking.

Truth, sincerity, authenticity, totality — these things should be the real concerns of morality. Consciousness, meditation, awareness, love, compassion — these should be the real concerns of morality.

But sex and morality became almost synonymous in the past; sex became overpowering, overwhelming. So whenever you say somebody is immoral you simply mean that something is wrong with his sexual life. And when you say somebody is a very moral person, all that you mean is that he follows the rules of sexuality laid down by the society in which he lives. Morality became one-dimensional; it has not been good. There is no future for that morality; that is dying. In fact, it is dead. You are carrying a corpse.

Sex should be more fun than such a serious affair as it has been made in the past. It should be like a game, a play: two persons playing with each other's bodily energies. If they both are happy, it should be nobody else's concern. They are not harming anybody; they are simply rejoicing in each other's energy. It is a dance of two energies together. It should not be a concern of the society at all. Unless somebody interferes in somebody else's life — imposes himself, forces somebody, is violent, violates somebody's life, then only should society come in. Otherwise there is no problem; it should not be any concern at all.

The future will have a totally different vision of sex. It will be more fun, more joy, more friendship, more a play than a serious affair as it has been in the past. It has destroyed people's lives, has burdened them so much — unnecessarily! It has created so much jealousy, possessiveness domination, nagging, quarrelling, fighting, condemnation — for *no* reason at all.

Not Knowing Is The Most Intimate

Sexuality is a simple, biological phenomenon. It should not be given so much importance. Its only significance is that the energy can be transformed into higher planes; it can become more and more spiritual. And the way to make it more spiritual is to make it a less serious affair.

Doctor Biber was perplexed by the case at hand. He had given the sorority girl all sorts of tests, but his results were still inconclusive. "I am not sure what it is," he finally admitted. "You either have a cold or you are pregnant."

"I must be pregnant," said the girl. "I don't know anybody who could have given me a cold."

This is something of the future.

Clarice and Sheffield were having a mid-afternoon breakfast. Their Park Avenue apartment was completely askew after a wild, all-night party.

"Dear, this is rather embarrassing," said Sheffield, "but was it you I made love to in the library last night?"

"About what time?" asked Clarice.

Another story about the future:

The schoolteacher was complaining rather bitterly to Cornelia about the behavior of little Nathaniel. "He is always picking on boys smaller than he is and beating them up," she said.

"My goodness!" said Cornelia, "That boy is just like his pappy."

"And several times I have caught him in the cloakroom with one of the little girls," continued the teacher.

"Just the sort of thing his pappy would do."

"Not only that, but he steals things from the other children."

"The very same as his pappy — Lord, I sure am glad I didn't marry that man!"

Don't be worried about the future of morality concerning sex. It is going to disappear completely. The future will know a totally different vision of sex. And once sex no longer overwhelms morality so powerfully, morality will be free to have some other concerns which are far more important.

Truth, sincerity, honesty, totality, compassion, service, meditation, these should be the real concerns of morality — because these are things which transform your life, these are things which bring you closer to God.

And the last question
Osho,

Why do you speak at all if the truth is inexpressible?

Paramahansa,
TAKE NO NOTICE!

An Invitation To Experience
OSHO
Never Born
Never Died
Only Visited This
Planet Earth Between
Dec 11, 1931 - Jan 19, 1990

Osho is an enlightened Mystic.

During the course of thirty years of talks to seekers and friends, Osho would answer their questions, or comment on the teachings of the world's great sages and scriptures. His talks continue to bring fresh insight to everything, from the obscure Upanishads to the familiar sayings of Gurdjieff, from Ashtavakra to Zarathustra. Osho speaks with equal authority on the Hassids and the Sufis, the Bauls, Yoga, Tantra, Tao and Gautama the Buddha. And ultimately, Osho concentrates on transmitting the unique wisdom of Zen, because, He says, Zen is the one spiritual tradition whose approach to the inner life of human beings has weathered the test of time and is still relevant to contemporary humanity. Zen is another word for the original Hindi word Dhyana. In English you may translate it as 'meditation', but Osho says this is a poor translation. So call it Dhyana or Zen or whatever you may wish - Osho's emphasis is on experiencing.

Osho settled in Pune in 1974, and disciples and friends from all over the world gathered around Him to hear His talks and practice His meditation techniques for the modern man. Western therapeutic group processes, classes and trainings were gradually introduced so bridging the wisdom and understanding of the East with the scientific approach of the West. And now Osho Commune International has evolved into the world's largest centre for meditation and spiritual growth, and offers hundreds of different methods for exploring and experiencing the inner world.

Every year, thousands of seekers from all over the world come to celebrate and meditate together in Osho's buddhafield. The commune grounds are full of lush green gardens, pools and waterfalls, elegant snow-white swans and colourful peacocks, as well as beautiful buildings and pyramids. Such a peaceful and harmonious atmosphere makes it very easy to experience the inner silence in a joyful way.

For detailed information to participate in this Buddhafield please contact:

OSHO COMMUNE INTERNATIONAL
17, Koregaon Park, Pune-411001, MS, India
Ph: 020 628562 Fax: 020 624181
E-mail: commune@osho.net Website: www.osho.com

BOOKS BY OSHO
English Language Editions

EARLY DISCOURSES AND WRITINGS
A Cup of Tea
Dimensions Beyond The Known
From Sex to Superconsciousness
The Great Challenge
Hidden Mysteries
I Am The Gate
The Inner Journey
The Long and the Short and the All
Psychology of the Esoteric
Seeds of Wisdom

MEDITATION
The Voice of Silence
And Now and Here (Vol 1 & 2)
In Search of the Miraculous (Vol 1 & 2)
Meditation: The Art of Ecstasy
Meditation: The First and Last Freedom
The Path of Meditation
The Perfect Way
Yaa-Hoo! The Mystic Rose

BUDDHA AND BUDDHIST MASTERS
The Book of Wisdom (combined edition of Vol 1 & 2)
The Dhammapada (Vol 1-12)
 The Way of the Buddha
The Diamond Sutra
The Discipline of Transcendence (Vol 1-4)
The Heart Sutra

BAUL MYSTICS
The Beloved (Vol 1 & 2)

KABIR
The Divine Melody
Ecstasy: The Forgotten Language
The Fish in the Sea is Not Thirsty
The Great Secret
The Guest
The Path of Love
The Revolution

JESUS AND CHRISTIAN MYSTICS
Come Follow to You (Vol 1-4)
I Say Unto You (Vol 1 & 2)
The Mustard Seed
Theologia Mystica

JEWISH MYSTICS
The Art of Dying
The True Sage

WESTERN MYSTICS
Guida Spirituale *On the Desiderata*

The Hidden Harmony
 The Fragments of Heraclitus
The Messiah (Vol 1 & 2) *Commentaries on Kahlil Gibran's The Prophet*
The New Alchemy: To Turn You On
 Commentaries on Mabel Collins' Light on the Path
Philosophia Perennis (Vol 1 & 2)
 The Golden Verses of Pythagoras
Zarathustra: A God That Can Dance
Zarathustra: The Laughing Prophet
 Commentaries on Nietzsche's Thus Spake Zarathustra

SUFISM
Just Like That
Journey to the Heart
 (same as Until You Die)
The Perfect Master (Vol 1 & 2)
The Secret
Sufis: The People of the Path (Vol 1 & 2)
Unio Mystica (Vol 1 & 2)
The Wisdom of the Sands (Vol 1 & 2)

TANTRA
Tantra: The Supreme Understanding
The Tantra Experience
 The Royal Song of Saraha
 (same as Tantra Vision, Vol 1)
The Tantric Transformation
 The Royal Song of Saraha
 (same as Tantra Vision, Vol 2)
The Book of Secrets: Vigyan Bhairav Tantra

THE UPANISHADS
Behind a Thousand Names
 Nirvana Upanishad
Heartbeat of the Absolute
 Ishavasya Upanishad
I Am That *Isa Upanishad*
The Message Beyond Words: A Dialogue with the Lord of Death
Philosophia Ultima *Mandukya Upanishad*
The Supreme Doctrine *Kenopanishad*
Finger Pointing to the Moon
 Adhyatma Upanishad
That Art Thou *Sarvasar Upanishad, KaivalyaUpanishad, Adhyatma Upanishad*
The Ultimate Alchemy
 Atma Pooja Upanishad (Vol 1 & 2)
Vedanta: Seven Steps to Samadhi
 Akshaya Upanishad

TAO
The Empty Boat
The Secret of Secrets
Tao: The Golden Gate (Vol 1 & 2)
Tao: The Pathless Path (Vol 1 & 2)
Tao: The Three Treasures (Vol 1-4)
When the Shoe Fits

YOGA
The Path of Yoga (previously Yoga: The Alpha and the Omega Vol 1)
Yoga: The Alpha and the Omega (Vol 2-10)

ZEN AND ZEN MASTERS
Ah, This!
Ancient Music in the Pines
And the Flowers Showered
A Bird on the Wing (same as Roots and Wings)
Bodhidharma: The Greatest Zen Master
Communism and Zen Fire, Zen Wind
Dang Dang Doko Dang
The First Principle
God is Dead: Now Zen is the Only Living Truth
The Grass Grows By Itself
The Great Zen Master Ta Hui
Hsin Hsin Ming: The Book of Nothing
 Discourses on the Faith-Mind of Sosan
I Celebrate Myself: God is No Where,
Life is Now Here
Kyozan: A True Man of Zen
Nirvana: The Last Nightmare
No Mind: The Flowers of Eternity
No Water, No Moon
One Seed Makes the Whole Earth Green
Returning to the Source
The Search: Talks on the 10 Bulls of Zen
A Sudden Clash of Thunder
The Sun Rises in the Evening
Take it Easy (Vol 1) *Poems of Ikkyu*
Take it Easy (Vol 2) *Poems of Ikkyu*
This Very Body the Buddha
 Hakuin's Song of Meditation
Walking in Zen, Sitting in Zen
The White Lotus
Yakusan: Straight to the Point of Enlightenment
Zen Manifesto : Freedom From Oneself
Zen: The Mystery and the

Poetry of the Beyond
Zen: The Path of Paradox
(Vol 1, 2 & 3)
Zen: The Special Transmission

ZEN BOXED SETS
The World of Zen (5 volumes)
- Live Zen
- This. This. A Thousand Times This
- Zen: The Diamond Thunderbolt
- Zen: The Quantum Leap from Mind to No-Mind
- Zen: The Solitary Bird, Cuckoo of the Forest

Zen: All The Colors Of The Rainbow (5 vol.)
- The Buddha: The Emptiness of the Heart
- The Language of Existence
- The Miracle
- The Original Man
- Turning In

Osho: On the Ancient Masters of Zen (7 vol.)
- Dogen: The Zen Master
- Hyakujo: The Everest of Zen— With Basho's Haikus
- Isan: No Footprints in the Blue Sky
- Joshu: The Lion's Roar
- Ma Tzu: The Empty Mirror
- Nansen: The Point Of Departure
- Rinzai: Master of the Irrational

Each volume is also available individually.

Responses to Questions
Be Still and Know
Come, Come, Yet Again Come
The Goose is Out
The Great Pilgrimage: From Here to Here
The Invitation
My Way: The Way of the White Clouds
Nowhere to Go But In
The Razor's Edge
Walk Without Feet, Fly Without Wings and Think Without Mind
The Wild Geese and the Water
Zen: Zest, Zip, Zap and Zing

Talks in America
From Bondage To Freedom
From Darkness to Light
From Death To Deathlessness
From the False to the Truth
From Unconsciousness to Consciousness
The Rajneesh Bible (Vol 2-4)

THE WORLD TOUR
Beyond Enlightenment *Talks in Bombay*
Beyond Psychology *Talks in Uruguay*
Light on the Path *Talks in the Himalayas*
The Path of the Mystic *Talks in Uruguay*
Sermons in Stones *Talks in Bombay*
Socrates Poisoned Again After 25 Centuries *Talks in Greece*
The Sword and the Lotus *Talks in the Himalayas*
The Transmission of the Lamp *Talks in Uruguay*

OSHO'S VISION FOR THE WORLD
The Golden Future
The Hidden Splendor
The New Dawn
The Rebel
The Rebellious Spirit

THE MANTRA SERIES
Hari Om Tat Sat
Om Mani Padme Hum
Om Shantih Shantih Shantih
Sat-Chit-Anand
Satyam-Shivam-Sundram

PERSONAL GLIMPSES
Books I Have Loved
Glimpses of a Golden Childhood
Notes of a Madman

INTERVIEWS WITH THE WORLD PRESS
The Last Testament (Vol 1)

INTIMATE TALKS BETWEEN MASTER AND DISCIPLE – DARSHAN DIARIES
A Rose is a Rose is a Rose
Be Realistic: Plan for a Miracle
Believing the Impossible Before Breakfast
Beloved of My Heart
Blessed are the Ignorant
Dance Your Way to God
Don't Just Do Something, Sit There
Far Beyond the Stars
For Madmen Only
The Further Shore
Get Out of Your Own Way
God's Got A Thing about You
God is Not for Sale
The Great Nothing
Hallelujah!
Let Go!
The 99 Names of Nothingness
No Book, No Buddha, No Teaching, No Disciple

Nothing to Lose but Your Head
Only Losers Can Win in This Game
Open Door
Open Secret
The Shadow of the Whip
The Sound of One Hand Clapping
The Sun Behind the Sun Behind the Sun
The Tongue-Tip Taste of Tao
This Is It
Turn On, Tune In and Drop the Lot
What Is, Is, What Ain't, Ain't
Won't You Join The Dance?

COMPILATIONS
After Middle Age: A Limitless Sky
At the Feet of the Master
Bhagwan Shree Rajneesh: On Basic Human Rights
Jesus Crucified Again, This Time in Ronald Reagan's America
Priests and Politicians: The Mafia of the Soul Take it Really Seriously

GIFT BOOKS OF OSHO QUOTATIONS
A Must for Contemplation Before Sleep
A Must for Morning Contemplation
India My Love

PHOTOBOOKS
Shree Rajneesh: A Man of Many Climates, Seasons and Rainbows through the eye of the camera
Impressions... Osho Commune International Photobook

BOOKS ABOUT OSHO
Bhagwan: The Buddha for the Future *by Juliet Forman*
Bhagwan Shree Rajneesh: The Most Dangerous Man Since Jesus Christ *by Sue Appleton*
Bhagwan: The Most Godless Yet the Most Godly Man *by Dr. George Meredith*
Bhagwan: One Man Against the Whole Ugly Past of Humanity *by Juliet Forman*
Bhagwan: Twelve Days That Shook the World *by Juliet Forman*
Was Bhagwan Shree Rajneesh Poisoned by Ronald Reagan's America? *by Sue Appleton*
My Diamond Days With Osho *by Ma Prem Shunyo*

GIFTS
Zorba the Buddha Cookbook

FULL CIRCLE publishes books on inspirational subjects, religion, philosophy, and natural health. The objective is to help make an attitudinal shift towards a more peaceful, loving, non-combative, non-threatening, compassionate and healing world.

FULL CIRCLE continues its commitment towards creating a peaceful and harmonious world and towards rekindling the joyous, divine nature of the human spirit.

Our fine books are available at all leading bookstores across the country.

FULL CIRCLE PUBLISHING

Registered Office
18-19, Dilshad Garden, G.T. Road, Delhi 110 095
Tel: 228 2467, 229 7792 • Fax: 228 2332

Editorial Office
J-40, Jorbagh Lane, New Delhi 110 003.
Tel : 461 5138, 462 0063 Fax: 464 5795

Bookstore
5B, Khan Market, New Delhi 110 003
Tel: 465 5641, 465 5642
email: fullcircle@vsnl.com